ABOUT THE
FOUNDATION FOR ENTERPRISE DEVELOPMENT

$\mathcal{T}$he mission of the Foundation for Enterprise Development is to develop productive, competitive enterprises by promoting entrepreneurial employee ownership and participation as a fair and effective means of motivating the workforce and improving corporate performance. By providing practical information and assistance to help organizations implement equity-based compensation and broad-based participation programs, the Foundation works to enhance economic and social development worldwide through broader ownership and involvement in the free enterprise system.

The Foundation was founded in 1986 by Dr. J. Robert Beyster, founder and Chairman and CEO of Science Applications International Corporation, one of the nation's largest employee-owned firms. Having experienced the power of employee ownership and participation first hand, Dr. Beyster was convinced that by sharing ownership and empowering employees, companies could compete more effectively in the world marketplace. The Foundation's activities focus on providing practical information and assistance to help companies implement effective equity compensation and employee involvement strategies.

FOUNDATION OFFICES

SAN DIEGO

P.O. Box 2149
La Jolla, CA 92038-2149
(t) 858.459.4662
(f) 858.459.6921
email: dsherman@fed.org

WASHINGTON D.C.

2020 K Street, NW, Suite 400
Washington DC 20006
(t) 202.530.8920
(f) 202.530.5702
email: dbinns@fed.org

This publication is intended to provide a summary of equity compensation methods and practical applications. The information contained herein does not constitute legal advice on the design or implementation of equity compensation plans, nor is it intended as a guide to implementation. Many features of equity compensation plan design and implementation need to be tailored on an individual basis. Professional legal, tax and accounting advice should be sought before designing or implementing any type of equity compensation plan.

TABLE OF CONTENTS

FOREWORD

INTRODUCTION

31911

FOREWORD

$\mathcal{T}$his updated and expanded edition of The Entrepreneur's Guide is designed to make equity compensation more relevant and understandable for all business executives. No matter whether a company is large or small, in a start-up, high growth or mature stage, or wanting executive-oriented or broad-based incentives, the business executive will find applicable approaches and principles inside.

New to this edition are additional examples, information related to tax law changes and new sections such as ESOPs and S Corporations and International Equity Compensation Plans.

The Foundation's vision for helping companies establish effective employee ownership plans is based on the leadership of Dr. J. Robert Beyster, founder, Chairman and CEO of Science Applications International Corporation, a $4 billion high technology company and one of the nation's largest employee-owned firms. Dr. Beyster began sharing stock ownership with employees upon SAIC's inception in 1969, because he felt it was only fair that those who contribute their energies to building the company should own it in a manner that is fair and consistent with their contribution. Convinced that employee ownership was the principal engine of SAIC's growth and success, Dr. Beyster started the Foundation for Enterprise Development in 1986 to help other companies use equity compensation methods effectively.

Over the past 12 years, staff at the Foundation has worked with hundreds of companies considering and implementing equity-based compensation plans. This book is the result of lessons learned and best practices from these consultations.

INTRODUCTION

One key challenge of any company owner/executive is to motivate his or her employees to work effectively toward the goals of growth and profitability. The ideal scenario is that every employee is cost conscious, understands the importance of customer satisfaction, looks for marketing and sales opportunities, and creates ways of doing his or her job more efficiently. In other words, every employee "thinks and acts like an owner." This book describes the methods by which companies enable employees to gain ownership in their company.

HOW TO USE THIS BOOK

This book is intended to serve as a reference and a guide for entrepreneurs, owners and executives who are contemplating using equity compensation in their company. We recommend that all readers review chapters I. The Equity Sharing Journey, IX. Critical Issues and X. Making Ownership Real. They describe elements that are essential to using any type of equity compensation program successfully. Readers should consult the Table of Contents, which highlights the key features of each equity sharing method, and so be able to pick and choose those methods of interest to them. Finally, readers may want to refer to the Appendix, which provides tables summarizing much of the research that has been conducted relating to employee ownership and participation.

Companies use equity compensation methods to achieve a variety of business objectives, such as recruiting and retention, reward for performance, employee motivation, and ownership transition. If done correctly, equity compensation can result in a win-win-win situation: The company is more productive and competitive; owners achieve liquidity or gain partners in making the company successful; and employees gain an ownership stake in their company, with the opportunity to use their talents and energies to enrich themselves and their co-workers.

KEY TERMS AND CONCEPTS

$\mathcal{T}$here are numerous terms and concepts referred to throughout this book. A brief introduction to some of them will provide context for the descriptions of equity methods that follow.

Qualified Plans vs. Non-qualified Plans:

Certain retirement plans qualify under specific sections of the Internal Revenue Code or ERISA for special deductions and/or income tax deferral. Typically, if an employee receives compensation, it is taxable to the employee and deductible to the corporation. Qualified plans allow the company to receive a current deduction for its contributions while allowing the employee to defer taxes until distribution. In order for a plan to "qualify," it must meet strict requirements regarding anti-discrimination. Qualified plans are therefore less flexible than non-qualified plans.

Defined Benefit Plan vs. Defined Contribution Plan:

A defined benefit retirement plan, also referred to as a pension plan, is a plan in which the employee's benefit is defined by the terms of the plan and is usually based on the employee's average salary during the last few years of work. The company is at risk for the plan asset investment and must ensure that the assets are sufficient to pay the defined benefit. A defined contribution plan is a plan in which the annual contribution level is defined by the plan and investment risk rests with the employee. The employee's retirement account is based on the pro rata contributions made to his or her individual account and the investment gains or losses on the account balance.

Restrictions:

Restrictions are rules that limit the transfer and sale of securities. One type of restriction is vesting, which lapses over time based on an employee's years of service with the company or based on meeting specific performance goals. Two other common restrictions are the right of repurchase at termination, which requires employees to sell their stock back to the company upon termination, and the right of first refusal, which gives the employer the right to match any offer to purchase the company's shares.

Liquidity:

Liquidity is the ability to exchange stock for cash. Without liquidity, or the understanding that liquidity will be provided at some time in the not-too-distant future, owning stock will have little meaning to employees. Non-publicly traded companies have a legal requirement to provide liquidity in the case of an ESOP, and a moral obligation to provide liquidity in the future for all other equity plans. Providing a liquidity mechanism is key to an effective equity program.

Theory of Constructive Receipt:

Under the theory of constructive receipt, an employee is subject to tax if he or she has unrestricted control in determining when income should be received. The intent of this concept is to prevent an employee from not accepting income that is unrestricted solely to avoid current taxation.

Economic Benefit Doctrine:

The economic benefit doctrine states that an employee is taxed when he or she receives something of value which is the equivalent of cash. Typically, a mere promise to pay in the future, if it is unfunded and unsecured, is not of sufficient economic benefit to be taxable even if it is non-forfeitable at the time it is made.

*T*he following are laws or governing bodies that regulate the use of equity compensation:

Internal Revenue Code/Regulations:
Enforced by the Internal Revenue Service (IRS), these laws determine the tax implications of different forms of compensation.

Employee Retirement Income Security Act (ERISA):
This 1974 act was designed to protect the rights of employees under tax qualified employee benefit plans. All qualified plans are subject to ERISA.

Securities and Exchange Acts:
The 1933 and 1934 acts set forth the principal federal rules governing the issue and sale of securities in the United States as enforced by the Securities and Exchange Commission (SEC). The 1933 act governs the sale of stock by a company to the public, while the 1934 act details the obligations on companies whose shares are held by the public. Both acts are guided by the general principle that a company may operate as it sees fit as long as it discloses all pertinent information to its shareholders.

Blue Sky Registration:
Blue Sky refers to state securities registration rules. Each state has separate registration rules with which a company must comply when issuing or selling stock to a citizen of that state.

Department of Labor (DOL):
This department of the Federal government was established to protect the rights of employees. The DOL gets involved in many employee benefit issues, including the voting of securities in benefit plans, employee participation committees and labor/management relations.

Financial Accounting Standards Board (FASB):
The FASB is the accounting profession's rule making body that determines how transactions regarding equity are to be reported on the books of the issuing corporation.

I. The Equity Sharing Journey

$\mathcal{M}$any factors influence the decision to establish equity-based compensation plans. However, the fundamental goal of most company owners and executives who adopt such plans is to give employees a financial and psychological stake in the success of the company. Equity compensation plans enable the sharing of ownership with employees, tying employees' long-term interests to the company's future. For this reason, these plans have the potential to create high performance organizations. But, turning this potential into reality requires careful attention to two factors: (1) designing an equity compensation strategy that meets company objectives, and (2) developing a culture that encourages employees to think and act like owners. This chapter addresses the first of these critical issues; Chapter X will address the other.

When James Kuhns, then with Sibson & Company, spoke at a Foundation conference, he summarized the basic premise of an equity compensation program:

> *"The system must enhance, reinforce, stimulate, advocate and reward accomplishments in support of the company's strategic and organizational direction, as well as its tactical milestones. It must also recognize the unique characteristics and nature of its operations and management environment. It must be in the real world, supported by an adequate information system, a realistic opportunity to impact results being measured, and a constructive management process."*

As Kuhns suggests, developing and maintaining an effective equity compensation program is an ongoing, long-term process that requires a significant investment of management time and corporate resources. Before describing various methods of equity compensation, it is important to understand the process by which companies develop equity compensation strategies.

Developing an equity compensation program is a combination of art and science. There is no cookie-cutter approach to designing and implementing an effective program. There are simply too many variables to be able to reduce equity compensation to a formula. However, after working with hundreds of companies, the Foundation has developed an eight step approach that provides guidance and direction for owners and executives interested in sharing stock ownership with employees.

Step 1: Define Your Vision and Objectives for Equity Sharing

The most critical step in developing an equity compensation plan is to define the business goals and objectives for the company and determine how the adoption of an equity compensation plan will support those objectives. The owner needs to answer the critical question: "What am I trying to achieve in my company by using equity compensation?" Possible answers include:

- Recruit and retain top performers
- Motivate employees to achieve business goals
- Reward employee performance with ownership
- Share ownership fairly with those who generate success
- Align employee interests with those of shareholders
- Raise capital
- Get all employees thinking and acting like owners
- Facilitate succession planning
- Buy out a departing owner on tax-advantaged terms
- Restructure the organization to better compete

- Finance an employee buyout
- Facilitate a corporate divestiture
- Protect against a takeover attempt
- Provide an attractive retirement benefit
- Restructure employee benefits programs

The owner must be as specific as possible when identifying the objectives that he or she is trying to achieve. Prioritizing these objectives will help determine which equity compensation strategies are most appropriate for the company.

WHAT SHOULD DRIVE EQUITY COMPENSATION PLAN DESIGN?

Three primary factors should drive equity compensation plan design. The first is the long-term strategy or ownership vision of the company. In other words, what is the long-term purpose of sharing ownership? For some companies, it may be quite pragmatic: *To attract and retain star employees to this new start-up, and keep them working extra hard so we can do an Initial Public Offering (IPO) in five years.* For others, it may be more philosophical: *To build a company that is employee-owned over the long-term, where those who work hardest are rewarded with a proportionate share of the equity, and where all employees are motivated to contribute to the long-term growth and success of the company.* A company's long-term strategy or ownership vision statement can serve as a reference point to measure success, and to make adjustments over time as the company's ownership structure evolves.

The second factor that drives equity compensation plan design has to do with the company's strategic business objectives. Over time strategic objectives change based on the growth stage of the company, the needs of its workforce, the competitive environment and other factors. Equity compensation plans can be refined to address the short-term strategic needs of the company, while still serving the long-term strategy or ownership vision. For example, in the start-up stage, a company's short-term objectives may be to attract key staff while conserving capital. Since the stock price is likely very low, the company may decide to offer key staff who join the company the opportunity to purchase an ownership position relatively cheaply and match shares purchased with restricted shares that vest over several years. Later, when the company has passed the start-up stage and is in the fast-growth mode, the focus of equity compensation may turn to stock option awards as a way to retain these key employees.

The third set of factors that drive equity compensation plan design are practical issues, which often provide limitations on how equity may be shared. Considerations like industry trends, workforce profile, tax and financial issues and the desires of current owners often weigh heavily in plan design. It is important to be aware of any issues that may impact plan design early in the equity compensation plan design process. Here are a few of the common issues:

Ownership: What is the current ownership structure of the company? Are current owners willing to sell some of their equity stake or dilute their ownership position? Is voting control an issue? What ownership stake will be made available and what is the expected value that will be created as a result? Since current owners must approve an equity sharing plan, it is important to have some projection of how equity compensation will be used to help the company meet future growth targets.

Capital: What is the capital structure of the company? Does the company need capital? Will the company be seeking outside investors in the near future? How will future investors view the equity compensation program?

Growth: What is the growth projection of the company? Is it a start-up with great growth potential? Is it young and in a fast-growth mode or is it a more established company with slower but steady growth? The risk factor and potential gains are important considerations with regard to employee participation in a stock program.

Culture: What is the company culture? Equity programs should be designed to reinforce the desired company culture. For example, individual performance-based equity incentives could be counterproductive in a company that is largely team based.

Workforce: What is the profile of the company's workforce? Age and education are factors that must be considered in developing the plan. For a young workforce, more immediate stock awards may provide greater motivation, whereas for an older workforce, providing equity through retirement vehicles may be appropriate. Education and availability of cash become factors for any company that plans to offer shares to employees for purchase.

Industry: What is the nature of the industry? What types of compensation programs are competitors using? In some industries, equity compensation is expected by employees as an industry standard; in others, employees may be skeptical.

STEP 2: ADDRESS YOUR FEARS AND CONCERNS ABOUT EQUITY SHARING

Chapter IX addresses many of the critical issues associated with implementing equity compensation plans. It's important for company owners to be knowledgeable about issues like securities registration, stock pricing, stock restrictions and liquidity options. Two of the most common concerns of company owners regarding equity sharing are dilution and control.

Some company owners believe it is important to maintain more than 50% ownership of the company in order to remain in control. Others owners believe that control has more to do with leadership than percent of outstanding shares owned. The differences between these two viewpoints are largely philosophical ones, and are best addressed by talking to other company owners who have dealt with this issue.

The issue of dilution is an important one to understand. For many entrepreneurs the key principle behind employee ownership ties closely with dilution. Advocates of employee ownership insist that while sharing ownership with employees dilutes current owners' percentage of the company owned, the increased employee productivity, motivation and retention that comes about with employee ownership increases the long-term value of the company and thus increases the value of current owners' equity. Much research has been conducted regarding the relationship between employee ownership and increased productivity and profitability. The most significant research findings show that there is a link between employee ownership and better company performance only where employee participation in company decision-making has been present. Additionally, research to track the stock price performance of public companies with at least 10 percent employee ownership has found that these companies' stock values have consistently outperformed the S&P 500 and Dow Jones Index over the past several years.

Nevertheless, it is important to understand the difference between the percent of shares owned and the economic value of one's ownership position. An owner might dilute his or her ownership percentage over time, but because of the increased value of the company, would enjoy a greater economic value while also sharing the wealth.

STEP 3: CHOOSE AN APPROACH TO EQUITY SHARING

There are three basic approaches to equity sharing. Identifying the approach most suited to a company's strategic needs will help the company's owners in designing an equity compensation plan. The first approach is performance-based incentives. Certain equity compensation tools like stock bonuses and restricted stock, direct stock purchase offers and stock options may be tailored to certain individuals or teams and may be linked with specific performance targets. These plans provide great flexibility and are relatively inexpensive to implement, though they require a greater degree of creative management as well.

The second approach is broad-based benefits, which are better suited to offering equity compensation to a broad cross-section of the workforce. This approach includes programs like the Section 423 Stock Purchase Plan, 401(k) plan and the non-leveraged Employee Stock Ownership Plan (ESOP). There are strict rules regarding how these plans may be structured, and they may not be tailored to specific individuals or teams based on performance.

The third approach to equity sharing is the leveraged ESOP, which is a powerful tool of corporate finance suited to meeting specific financial objectives of the company or its owners and which provides for broad-based employee ownership. A leveraged ESOP enables employees to finance the purchase of company stock, backed by the corporation's guarantee, with the debt repaid out of future corporate earnings.

Because each of these approaches is best suited to different objectives, it may help to look at the chart below to determine which approach(es) best fits your company's objectives.

COMPARING APPROACHES BY OBJECTIVES

KEY: Y= YES
N= NO
M=MAYBE

	PERFORMANCE BASED	BROAD BASED	LEVERAGED ESOP
Reward all based on company performance	M	Y	Y
Offer stock as a part of compensation	Y	M	N
Reward group/team performance	Y	N	N
Create an "ownership culture"	M	Y	Y
Provide a retirement benefit	N	Y	Y
Sell part of the company	N	N	Y
Raise capital	M	M	Y
Cash out a shareholder	N	N	Y
Lead an employee buyout	N	N	Y
Recruit and retain employees	Y	N	N
Borrow on a tax favored basis	N	N	Y
Reward individual performance	Y	N	N
Encourage all employees to buy stock	N	Y	N
Provide incentives for performance goals	Y	M	N

STEP 4: EVALUATE THE VARIOUS EQUITY COMPENSATION METHODS AND SELECT THE BEST FOR YOU

Chapters II-VIII provide a description of the different methods of equity compensation available to a company — stock purchase programs, stock bonus awards, stock option plans, 401(k) and other qualified retirement plans, ESOPs and nonqualified deferred compensation — and some of the innovative ways in which plans can be designed. Companies may want to use one or several of these methods.

Based on the business objectives and company profile, several equity options should emerge as best suited to a company's particular needs. Evaluating each from the perspective of its operational dynamics may provide useful insight into which equity compensation method(s) to use.

Overall objective of the plan: benefit versus incentive versus investment - Retirement plans, such as ESOPs and 401(k) plans, are often viewed as long-term benefits by employees, and may not provide strong enough incentive for meeting performance objectives as compared to more immediate awards of stock options and stock bonuses. On the other hand, long-term benefits that provide an ownership stake to employees can be an important means of bonding employees to the company and instilling a sense of pride and loyalty. Plans enabling employees to make a cash investment, such as stock purchase plans and 401(k) plans where company stock is an investment choice, have a different psychological impact. Many people believe that when employees invest some of their hard-earned cash to purchase stock, it is more meaningful than stock ownership that is given to them as a benefit. Employees who make a conscious choice to invest in the company may arguably be more interested in the company's financial performance and stock returns.

Type of ownership: direct versus indirect - With stock option plans, stock bonus awards and stock purchase plans, the shares are held directly by employees. With retirement plans such as ESOPs and 401(k) plans, the stock is held in a trust for the benefit of employees. In the latter, a trustee votes the employees' shares, although the plan may provide for pass-through voting, whereby plan participants provide the trustee with instructions as to how to vote the shares in their individual accounts. With direct plans, employees typically gain all rights to voting, sharing of information, etc.

Ownership participation: targeted versus broad-based - Certain plans, such as stock option plans, stock bonus plans and direct stock purchase offers enable management, by formula or by discretion, to provide equity awards based on individual, team or group performance. Other plans, such as ESOPs and 401(k) plans with a stock match, work well for sharing equity broadly among employees. Section 423 stock purchase plans, and 401(k) plans in which company stock is an investment option, are also broad-based, but enable employees to make their own investment decision to purchase stock in their company.

Timing of performance incentives: before-the-fact versus after-the-fact - When equity awards are intended to reward performance, it is important to consider whether to reward employees based on their performance after the fact (with no prior knowledge of award level), or whether to require employees to meet pre-established performance objectives in order to receive certain levels of equity awards. One says, "thanks for a great job," and the other says, "if you can achieve these goals, you will be rewarded at these levels."

Award basis: individual versus team/group versus company - Performance-based rewards can be offered based on individual performance, team or group performance, project performance, company performance or any combination of factors. Ownership can also be shared evenly based on company performance. How equity awards are determined, communicated and distributed sends a message to employees about how they are expected to perform.

There are many other design factors to consider at this stage relating to the size, length, and pricing of awards as well as the restrictions to attach to them. It is important to revisit the objectives defined in Step 1 to ensure that the program's design meets the company's objectives.

STEP 5: MAP OUT YOUR EQUITY COMPENSATION PLAN

This step involves mapping out an equity compensation plan taking into consideration the potential positive and negative impacts of the program on the company and employees. Factors to consider:

Cost: Are these programs cost effective to implement and administer? Are there costs to employees and if so, are they prohibitive and therefore restrict participation?

Tax: What are the available tax incentives for the company and employees? It is important to balance the company's financial interests with the impact on the program's effectiveness as a result of tax consequences to employees. This is particularly relevant when there is no ready market for employees to cash in shares to cover the potential tax liability.

Financial: How will the proposed methods affect the company's financial statements? How will they be expected to boost financial performance? Will the plan result in equity dilution or will shares be purchased from existing shareholders?

Motivation: How will the program be perceived by employees? Is it designed to reinforce the company culture and reward behaviors critical to the company's future success? Will it be perceived by most employees as fair? This is a particularly good stage to get feedback from employees on the proposed program.

Management Support: What are the attitudes of current owners, directors and managers towards employee ownership and how that will affect corporate operations?

Control Issues: Are there concerns about the potential changes in the distribution of ownership and voting control? Financial disclosure and stockholder rights (voting and access to information in particular) required by plan design should be discussed with current owners, managers and directors.

Communications: How will the plan and the reasoning behind implementing it be communicated to employees? A comprehensive communications plan should be developed with the involvement and leadership of top management and other key employees.

Employee Involvement: To what degree is employee involvement in operations planned to be closely coupled with equity sharing?

There are also other critical issues, detailed further in Chapter IX, relating to securities registration, financial disclosure, stock pricing, stock restrictions and liquidity.

STEP 6: TEST YOUR APPROACH

The final step prior to implementation is to test your approach. This simply means giving it a "sanity check" by talking about it to your employees, colleagues and professional advisors. The Foundation for Enterprise Development is another excellent resource. The Foundation provides free advisory services to owners on this topic. The reason it is important to give your plan one last review is that sometimes along the path of considering all of the approaches and critical issues, business owners lose sight of the primary objectives behind implementing the plan. It is always good practice to ask yourself one final time: "Will this plan meet my strategic objectives?"

STEP 7: IMPLEMENT YOUR PLAN

At this point, owners and executives should work with attorneys, financial advisors, accountants, benefits consultants and possibly investment bankers to iron out the details and implement the program. Companies should begin rolling out a communications program, which will be critical to the plan's success. Employees want to know the "why" behind equity compensation in addition to the "how."

Step 8: Re-evaluate Your Program and Adjust

Maintaining an effective equity compensation plan requires constant evaluation of the program. The best method to evaluate the program is to revisit the original objectives of the plan and solicit employee and management feedback to determine if it is accomplishing the desired results. Other indicators include improved financial performance, turnover rates, employee morale and employee capital accumulation. Over time, the rationale for the program may change based on internal dynamics, the marketplace or other factors. It may be necessary to adjust the program over time to accommodate changing circumstances and/or objectives of the company and its workforce.

II. Stock Purchase Programs

$\mathcal{S}$tock purchase programs provide employees with the opportunity to participate more fully in long-term company growth, and are increasingly popular because of the belief that stock ownership is more meaningful to employees when they have invested their own money. This chapter addresses two of the most common types of purchase plans - direct stock purchase plans and Section 423 "discount purchase" plans. Both types can be inexpensive to set up and simple to administer, but are used to meet very different objectives.

Direct purchase plans are very flexible and can be tailored to a select group of employees. They can be used to enable top performers to become owners, to require senior managers to invest in the company or, in a start-up situation, to ensure the commitment of founding employees.

Section 423 "Discount Purchase" plans give employees the chance to purchase company stock through payroll deductions at a small discount. They are best suited to companies that want to encourage broad-based investment and equity participation.

Any time a company offers stock for sale to employees, securities laws (federal and state) must be carefully considered. While there are many exemptions available, securities laws are complex and therefore a securities attorney should be consulted.

Comparison of Direct Purchase and Section 423 Plan

Direct stock purchase plans	Section 423 discount purchase plans
Discretionary offer to selected employees	Virtually all employees must be allowed to participate
Flexible pricing is allowed	Price must be based on fair market value
Unlimited discount allowed	Discount limited to 15% of price at beginning or end of offering period
Discount taxable to recipient at grant; deduction for company	Discount not taxable to recipient at grant; no deduction for company
Securities registration may be required if offering is significant	Exemptions from securities registration may be available
Payroll withholding via company loan is possible	Payroll withholding
Not subject to ERISA	Not subject to ERISA

Direct Stock Purchase Plans

How they work

Direct stock purchase plans are simply offers made to employees to purchase a stated number of shares of stock. The company may make a loan to the employee, thus allowing him or her to pay for the purchase over time. In some cases, the purchase price may be discounted, or the company may match a purchase with stock options or a stock bonus in order to make the purchase offer more attractive to the employee.

Because variations in designing direct stock purchase plans are almost limitless, these plans can be tailored to address the particular financial, tax and other strategic needs of the company and its employees. The main limitation on direct stock purchase plans is generally imposed by securities registration, although exemptions are available depending upon the company's circumstances.

CREATIVE APPLICATIONS

Ownership Guidelines: A major trend occurring in both public and private companies is the requirement that senior executives have a significant investment in the company. In certain cases, executives are required to own a multiple of salary (1 to 5 times) or a total number of shares of company stock, with higher ownership requirements corresponding to increased job responsibility. These plans are sometimes called Employee Targeted Ownership Plans (ETOPs). Along with direct stock purchase plans, a company may establish other equity compensation plans in which the executive can participate in order to meet the guideline requirements.

Purchase Plans for Start-ups: To foster commitment and to allow potential stock gains to be eligible for capital gains tax treatment, many companies in the start-up phase will give employees the opportunity to purchase shares of common stock in the company. Because of the risk involved in start-up companies and because common stock typically has lesser voting and liquidation rights compared to preferred stock, the shares can usually carry a very low price. In virtually all cases, vesting schedules are attached to the shares, requiring the employee to stay with the company for a number of years (typically four) to benefit from the appreciation on the stock. If the employee terminates employment prior to vesting of the stock, the plan would provide for the company to purchase those shares back from the employee at the price the employee paid. In this situation it is extremely important that the employee files a section 83(b) election ensuring that any future appreciation in shares is not taxable for the employee until the stock is sold. For many early stage start-up companies, particularly those intending to do an Initial Public Offering, stock purchase plans can be preferable to stock option plans.

Discounted Stock Purchases: offer employees the ability to purchase stock at a discount, sometimes with conditions attached such as restrictions on transfer or the required purchase of additional stock. This provides an incentive for key employees to purchase stock in the company, gaining employee buy-in and commitment to the long term growth of the organization. Any discount requires the company to expense the value of the discount on its books for accounting purposes and may trigger taxation for the employees.

A Book Value Plan: is an alternate pricing method for discounting the purchase of stock. This method is generally used if no fair market valuation is available. Stock is sold at a purchase price equal to current book value or a multiple thereof, with a provision for the company's repurchase of the stock at the current book value in effect when the employee retires or leaves the company. The employee is not taxed on any increase in the stock value until the stock is sold. The employee also receives dividends and voting privileges while the stock is held during employment.

Matching Awards: Stock purchase offers can be tied to an employee meeting specific performance objectives. When used this way, the purchase offer may be matched with bonus shares or stock options, with vesting tied to either type of matching award.

TAX AND COST IMPLICATIONS

Tax treatment of direct stock purchase plans depends on the features of the particular plan, but generally, discounts result in ordinary income to the employee based on the difference between fair market value at the date of purchase and the purchase price. The employer receives a corresponding tax deduction when the employee realizes the income. If the sale of discounted stock is restricted, for example, through vesting for example, tax will be deferred until the restrictions lapse, unless a section 83(b) election has been made. (See page 16 on section 83 (b) elections.)

Section 1202 of the Internal Revenue Code allows employees to pay tax at a rate of only 14% on the capital gains on the sale of stock of qualifying small businesses if the stock is held by the employee for at least five years and certain other conditions are met.

A direct purchase plan is one of the most inexpensive to implement. Implementation costs could run as low as $1,000 - $3,000. The primary cost is in developing a shareholder agreement which should outline stock restrictions, stock pricing and any other conditions on the shares offered to each employee.

CAPITAL GAINS EXCLUSION FOR SMALL BUSINESSES

Qualified small business stock is limited to stock issued after August 10, 1993.

The issuer must be a domestic C-corporation that does not have more than $50 million in aggregate gross assets, including amounts received upon issuance of the stock. Gross assets means cash and the adjusted basis of other property.

Certain businesses are not qualified small businesses, including any business involving the performance of services in the fields of health, law, engineering, architecture, accounting, actuarial science, performing arts, consulting, athletics, financial services, brokerage services, banking, insurance, financing, leasing, investing, farming, mineral extraction, and operating a hotel, motel, restaurant or similar business. The company must also satisfy certain "active" business requirements through the five year holding period.

There are many technicalities related to this special tax deduction. Companies should consult with their tax advisors to determine if they qualify. For companies that qualify, special consideration should be given to the design of equity programs. For example, the five-year holding period begins upon exercise, not grant, of a stock option; upon vesting of restricted stock; or upon filing of a section 83(b) election.

ACCOUNTING CONSIDERATIONS

For financial accounting purposes, most direct purchase plans are considered compensatory, requiring the employer to expense the value of any discount on the purchase price in the year of purchase. If the stock is sold at a price equal to fair market value, no compensation expense is required.

SECTION 423 DISCOUNT PURCHASE PLANS

HOW THEY WORK

Section 423 discount purchase plans are set up to allow a broad-based group of employees to purchase company stock and give employees an incentive to invest in their company. Most plans are structured to allow employees to use payroll withholding to purchase the shares. Contributions are accumulated and used to purchase stock on specific dates. Because of this delay the actual purchase is considered to be a stock option.

The option price and the offering period are variables under each plan. Some employers establish the price at fair market value at the date the stock is purchased. Others establish a price that is the lower of the price at the beginning or the end of the offering period. In most cases, the company allows the employee to purchase stock at a discounted price, which, under provisions of section 423, cannot be less than 85% of fair market value of the stock at the beginning or the end of the offering period.

The option period is partly determined by the option price. If the option price is at least 85% of the fair market value of the company stock at the time the option is exercised, i.e., the stock is purchased, the option period cannot exceed five years. If the option price is set in any other manner, the option period cannot exceed 27 months. The majority of plans have an option period of two years or less; most are set at six months or one year.

Section 423 discount purchase plans must be approved by shareholders and are only available to current employees. Generally, all employees must be allowed to participate, but employees who own 5% or more of the employer's stock are excluded from participation. Anytime a company sells stock to employees, securities registration requirements must be carefully analyzed and available exemptions considered.

HOW A SECTION 423 DISCOUNT PURCHASE WOULD WORK

ASSUMPTIONS:
- 1 Year Stock Offering Period
- Purchase price set at 85% of the lower of fair market value of stock at the time the option is granted or fair market value at time the stock is purchased.
- John has $850 withheld from his pay check over the stock option period to purchase stock:

Jan. 1	Dec. 31
Date of Grant	Exercise Date
FMV = $10.00/Share	FMV = $15.00/Share

The Plan purchases 100 shares of stock for John on Dec. 31 for $8.50/Share (85% x $10.00)

(If the share price had declined to $9.00/share ton Dec. 31, he plan would have purchased 111 shares at $7.65/share.)

KEY SECTION 423 PLAN REQUIREMENTS

Section 423 plans are required to grant purchase rights to all employees who meet all of the following stipulations:

- have been an employee with the company for at least 2 years
- work at least 20 hours per week
- work a minimum of five months per calendar year.

The share price can be no less than the lower of 85% of fair market value of the stock at the time the option is granted or at the time the option is exercised.

Employees holding 5% or more of company stock are not eligible to participate.

TAX AND COST IMPLICATIONS

There is no taxable event to the employee at the date of grant or the date the stock is purchased. The employee must recognize income at the date the stock is sold. If the employee acquired stock at less than 100% of the fair market value at the time the price was set, he or she must recognize compensation income on the amount of the discount at the time of sale. The tax basis in the stock acquired would be increased by the amount of compensation income recognized. Capital gains would be based on the difference between the proceeds received on the sale and the new tax basis.

The employer is not entitled to deduct the amount of the discount unless the employee sells the stock within the minimum statutory holding period. The holding period is two years from the date the stock is granted and one year after the stock is purchased by the employee.

EXAMPLE OF A SECTION 423 TRANSACTION

On January 1, all employees of X Corporation are given the opportunity to participate in the new stock purchase plan. The plan sets the price of the stock at 85% of the lower of the price at the beginning of the year or the end of the purchase year. The price is $10.00/share on Jan 1 and $15.00/Share on Dec. 31. Employee A exercised 100 options on Dec. 31 and purchases 100 shares of stock at $8.50/share (85% of $10.00). He holds the stock for three years and then sells it for $20.00/Share. Employee A would be required to recognize compensation income equal to $150 at the date of sale (the difference between the $10.00 FMV of the stock at the time the price is set and the $8.50 paid for the stock multiplied by the 100 shares purchased). Employee A would also recognize capital gains of $1,000 (the difference of the $2,000 proceeds on the sale of the stock and the new basis of the stock of $1,000, calculated by adding the $150 of compensation income to the $850 exercise price). The Corporation would receive no tax deduction on this transaction because employee A held the stock for over two years from the date of grant and one year from the date of purchase. If Employee A sold the stock within one year of the date he/she purchased the stock, Corporation X would be entitled to a $150 deduction, equal to the amount of compensation income Employee A was required to recognize.

Section 423 plans are relatively inexpensive and simple to set up. Legal costs may run as low as $2,000 - $5,000, although because most plans are administered by an outside organization, administration costs may run as high as $1,000 - $3,000 per year, depending on the number of employees participating.

ACCOUNTING CONSIDERATIONS

For accounting purposes, employers do not have to recognize a compensation expense for sales of stock, including the discount, under Section 423 discount purchase plans. The discount must be booked as a reduction in shareholder equity.

ADVANTAGES AND DRAWBACKS

Both direct purchase plans and Section 423 plans have the following advantages and drawbacks:

ADVANTAGES

Make ownership meaningful: Stock ownership is generally considered to be more meaningful to employees who have invested their own funds to acquire the shares.

Align interests of employees and shareholders: Through stock purchases, employees become investors in the company and thus become more aligned with the goals and objectives of other shareholders.

Generate capital: All stock purchase plans generate some capital for the company, although companies should generally not depend on their employees to generate significant capital.

DRAWBACKS

Cost of investment may deter participation: Employees who have to come up with cash or reduce their paychecks to invest in the company may be less likely to do so.

Securities issues: For non-publicly traded companies, the sale of stock to employees may raise significant legal and administrative requirements with respect to compliance with federal and state securities registration laws though exemptions to securities requirements are available (see details on page 59).

III. Stock Bonus Awards

Stock bonus awards are one of the simplest and most flexible ways to provide employees a stake in your company's future growth. Bonus award plans can be tailored to reward performance, link executive compensation with the long-term success of the company, provide incentives for employees to stay with the company, attract key personnel, and supplement other forms of bonus, incentive, or retirement compensation. Low setup costs and ease of implementation make stock bonus award programs attractive to companies of all sizes as a means of sharing equity with employees.

How They Work

There are two main types of stock bonus award programs:

Non-Restrictive Stock Bonus: An outright award of stock, usually given to key employees for achieving financial or strategic goals. This award acts like a cash bonus except that the award is in stock rather than cash.

Restricted Stock Bonus: An award subject to conditions, such as requiring employees to stay with the company over a period of years (vesting) or meeting specific performance requirements before realizing the full benefit of the award.

Both types of bonus awards can be tailored to meet specific company objectives. For example, a company might structure a bonus plan to reward certain employees or business sectors for bringing in new business, managing a project under budget or meeting project goals. A company might also provide stock bonuses to employees who purchase stock, thereby giving them a greater incentive to buy. A start-up company might provide stock bonus awards as part of an employee's annual compensation, thereby saving needed cash. Stock offered with an attached vesting schedule can be an effective vehicle in retaining employees, particularly if awards are made annually rather than just once.

Since a stock bonus results in a tax liability for the employee, it can cause negative cash flow implications for the employee. Therefore, some companies also provide a cash bonus award to the employee (which is also taxable) to offset taxes required to be paid on the stock portion of the bonus.

Vesting restrictions on stock bonus awards can end all at once (cliff vesting), or in installments over a period of time with some provision for accelerated vesting for meeting specific performance targets or in the event of death, disability, retirement or a change in control of the company.

Example of a
Non-Restrictive Stock Bonus Award

Because you achieved outstanding success during this past year you have been awarded a stock bonus of 200 shares of company stock valued at $10.00/share.

In addition, to help offset taxes, you have been awarded a $1,000 cash bonus. (The total value of the bonus, $3,000, is taxable income to you.)

TAX AND COST IMPLICATIONS

Tax implications for non-restrictive stock bonuses are straightforward. For the employee, the fair market value (FMV) of the stock is taxed as ordinary income. The company receives a tax deduction equal to the amount of income the employee must recognize. The company is responsible for withholding employment taxes from the employee. This can be done either by a lump-sum withholding at the time of the award or by spreading the deduction among future pay periods during the current tax year.

A different set of tax rules applies to restricted stock bonuses. For income tax purposes, the employee is generally treated as receiving ordinary income at the date the restrictions lapse and the stock is no longer subject to a substantial risk of forfeiture. The amount recognized as ordinary income is equal to the fair market value of the stock on the date that the restrictions lapse.

To avoid being taxed at ordinary income tax rates for expected future increases in the value of the stock, an employee may elect under Section 83(b) of the Internal Revenue Code to pay taxes based on the stock value in the year it is awarded. If and when the stock becomes vested, the employee does not pay tax on any increases in the stock value. That increase in value is taxed at capital gains rates when the stock is sold. Accordingly, a Section 83(b) election converts a portion of what would otherwise be ordinary income into capital gains income.

Section 83(b) also creates some risk for the employee. If the employee forfeits the stock for any reason (such as terminating service before vesting lapses), he or she will not be entitled to a refund of taxes paid. If the value of the stock decreases after a Section 83(b) election is made, upon its sale the decrease in value will be characterized as capital and be subject to the capital loss limitation rules, with the higher taxes paid not recovered.

EXAMPLE

ASSUMPTIONS:
- Employee receives stock bonus of 100 shares on Jan 1, Year 1, when the FMV of the stock is $10/share.
- The stock value increases 20% per year.
- Ordinary income tax rate 28%, capital gains rate 20%.
- The stock award vests at 25% per year.
- The stock is sold in year 6 for $25/share.

	No Section 83(b) election	Section 83(b) election
Taxes Paid Yr. 1	$0	$280
2	$84*	0
3	$101	0
4	$121	0
5	$145	0
6	$178	$300
Total Taxes Paid	$629	$580

*(25 x12) x 28%, representing 25 vested shares, multiplied by $12/share, the new FMV of stock in Year 2, multiplied by the ordinary income tax rate of 28%.

The most advantageous uses of a Section 83(b) election are (1) when there is potential for large stock price increases over the vesting period (as in start-up or fast-growth companies) and (2) where an employee is likely to stay with the company throughout the vesting period.

ADVANTAGES OF THE 83(B) ELECTION

- The employee pays compensation income tax on all of the value of the stock at grant, without regard to the restrictions. If the stock increases in value during the restricted period, there is no additional tax when the restrictions lapse.
- When the stock is sold, increase in value will be treated as capital gains rather than ordinary income.
- The holding period for capital gains treatment begins in the year the 83(b) election is made.
- The company is entitled to a compensation expense deduction at the same time and in the same amount as the employee's compensation income tax liability.

DISADVANTAGES OF THE 83(B) ELECTION

- If the stock is forfeited, there is no refund, tax credit or deduction allowed for the tax already paid.
- Tax liability is immediate, rather than deferred.
- Risk of stock decreasing in value creating an overpayment of taxes.

Stock bonus plans are fairly simple to establish and administer. Because they do not involve an offer to sell stock, stock bonus plans are generally exempt from SEC registration requirements. The cost to implement a stock bonus plan may run $2,000 - $5,000. Typically, administration costs are low, since most plans can be administered internally.

ADVANTAGES AND DRAWBACKS
Stock Bonus Plans

ADVANTAGES

Simple to establish and understand

Puts ownership directly into the hands of the employees

May be tailored to meet many different corporate objectives

There is no legal requirement for an independent appraisal of stock

Flexibility with regard to selection of recipients and size of awards

DRAWBACKS

Gives immediate ownership and voting rights to employees

Increases outstanding shares and therefore cash requirements for potential share repurchases for non-public companies

Since no investment is required, employees may not fully appreciate the ownership value

Tax liability to employee for non-cash award

INNOVATIVE APPROACHES

Following are some innovative variations of stock bonus awards:

Use of stock bonus awards to provide incentives for employees to purchase additional stock.

Vesting or outright stock award, tied to meeting specific corporate goals. These goals could include bringing in new business, completing projects under budget or in a timely manner, or meeting certain quality standards.

ACCOUNTING CONSIDERATIONS

Generally, the compensation expense that must be accounted for is the market value of the stock at grant. This amount is charged to earnings over the restricted period. However, if vesting is based on performance objectives, compensation expense is adjusted each year as the stock price changes until the vesting actually occurs. Earnings per share are often diluted when restricted stock is granted, since this involves the issuance of actual shares, usually with dividend and voting rights. The extent of the dilution is calculated in a manner similar to stock options.

IV. Stock Option Plans

Stock options are one of the most widely used methods of providing employees with an opportunity to acquire an equity interest in their employer. The popularity of stock options is due primarily to the flexibility and low carrying costs from an employee perspective. In addition, they are not overly complicated to establish and maintain, and receive favorable accounting treatment. Stock options are particularly useful for smaller companies or start-ups that want to provide incentives for individual employees or use stock as a form of compensation while preserving cash during the early stages of the company's growth. The exercise of options also brings capital into the company. In addition, companies use stock options to recruit, retain and motivate their staffs. At any stage of a company's growth, stock options provide an effective opportunity for employees to participate in the increased value they help generate and thus help align employee interests with those of the shareholders.

Stock Options at a Glance

Stock options are one of the most flexible equity compensation methods and one of the least expensive to implement and administer.

Option grants give employees a low risk opportunity to participate in the future success of the company and become owners.

Options are attractive from an accounting standpoint since generally no compensation expense is required.

Stock options generate capital for the company and reinforce employee buy-in through investment in the company.

Stock options have typically been reserved for key employees - usually owners and top executives. Although this practice still remains, particularly among privately held companies, more and more companies are creating programs that provide a broad base of employees with opportunities to acquire shares on option, thus recognizing the valuable contribution that all employees make to the company and spreading the incentive of ownership more broadly throughout the organization.

How They Work

A stock option is a contract between the company and the employee giving the employee the right to purchase shares of company stock within certain dates, at a price that is fixed by the company or determinable by a formula defined at the time the option is granted. Because employees are not bound to purchase the stock, there is no risk of loss to the employee prior to exercising options. If the value of the stock increases after the date the options are granted, then the employee may acquire the shares at the value fixed at the time of grant, thereby acquiring stock at potentially significant discounts.

For example, a company issues an option to an employee allowing the employee to purchase 100 shares of stock at the current stock price of $1 per share. The option term period is five years, meaning that the employee has five years in which to exercise the option and pay for the stock. If the stock price increases to $5 per share by the end of the five-year period, the employee could exercise the option by paying $100 for shares worth $500. If the price decreases after the option is granted, the employee would forgo exercising the option, and thereby have no financial loss.

Stock options typically require employees to pay the exercise price in cash and to pay any withholding taxes due on the option gain. The employee can either perceive this outlay as a positive (a personal investment in the company) or a negative (if the employee cannot afford it or is risk-averse). To reduce or eliminate the cash outlay by employees, many companies allow employees to exercise their options through a "stock for stock" transaction or a "cashless exercise." Stock for stock transactions enable employees to pay the exercise price (and, in some cases, required withholding taxes) with stock they already own. However, shares used by the employee to exercise an option must be owned for at least six months in order to be used to cover the exercise price. In "cashless exercise" programs, the employee borrows money from a broker to exercise the option and immediately sells some of the shares to pay back the exercise price plus any taxes and commissions. Using cashless exercises or stock for stock transactions, the employee ends up holding shares representing the value of the spread between the exercise price and the fair market value at the date of exercise, less any taxes paid on the transaction. In addition, some companies also permit selected employees to borrow money from the company (typically secured by the purchased stock) to pay the exercise price.

TWO TYPES OF OPTIONS

There are two types of stock options - Incentive Stock Options (ISOs) and Non-qualified Stock Options (NSOs). ISOs offer tax incentives to the optionee, but are less flexible for the company in terms of plan design. In addition, there are numerous conditions a plan must meet to receive the positive tax treatment of an ISO.

SUMMARY OF ISO REQUIREMENTS

- Option price cannot be less than 100% of fair market value at the grant date
- Aggregate face value of options that may become exercisable by any one individual in any one year is limited to $100,000, measured at the date of grant
- For shareholders owning 10% or more of voting stock, option price may not be less than 110% of fair market value
- To receive favorable tax treatment, optionee must hold shares acquired through an ISO for two years after the grant date and one year after the exercise date
- ISOs must be granted under a written plan approved by shareholders
- Plan must specify total number of shares that may be issued and class of employees eligible for option grants
- ISOs may be granted only to employees (not consultants or non-employee directors)
- Option term may not exceed 10 years (5 years for 10% shareholders)
- ISOs may not be transferred

NSOs are options that do not meet the specific requirements of an ISO. For example, if the exercise price of an option is less than the fair market value of the underlying stock when the option is granted, then the stock option must be characterized as an NSO. Because they are less tax-advantaged, there are no design requirements imposed on NSOs by the Internal Revenue Code, although state securities requirements may impose certain design limitations on NSOs. ISOs that are exercised and sold prior to the end of the required holding period are generally taxed like NSOs.

TAX AND COST IMPLICATIONS

At the time when options are granted to employees, there is no tax consequence for either the employer or the employee. However, the tax treatment that occurs at the exercise date and disposition (sale) date differs, depending upon whether the option is an ISO or an NSO.

With an NSO, on the exercise date the employee must generally pay tax (ordinary income) on the difference between the exercise price and the current stock price. The company receives a corresponding deduction. Upon sale of the stock, the employee must pay capital gains tax on the difference between the stock price on the exercise date and the sale price.

With an ISO, the employee does not pay regular income tax upon exercise, but instead defers recognition of the gain until the stock is sold, at which time the total gain, i.e., the difference between the proceeds on the sale and the price paid at exercise, is taxed at capital gain rates. The gain at the exercise date may, however, cause the employee to pay some federal alternative minimum taxes (AMT). With an ISO, the company does not receive a deduction unless the employee fails to hold the stock for the holding period required to receive tax favored treatment, i.e., two years from grant, one year from exercise. In such a case the corporate tax deduction is equal to the gain at the exercise date, i.e., the difference between the price paid and the fair market value at the exercise date. Upon the sale of the stock after satisfying the holding period, the employee pays capital gains tax on the difference between the exercise price and the sale price. No corporate tax deduction is recorded.

While NSOs offer more flexibility of design, ISOs can generate capital gains and thus can provide a tax savings (and deferral) to employees relative to NSOs. Careful analysis of the tradeoffs on employee and employer tax implications should be done before choosing which type to implement.

ILLUSTRATION OF TAX IMPLICATIONS OF ISOs VERSUS NSOs

ASSUMPTIONS:
- Mary receives 200 option shares
- Grant price of $10/share (FMV)
- Option term is 5 years
- Stock price is $15/share in year 5 when Mary exercises
- Stock price is $20/share in year 10 when Mary sells

	ISO	NSO
At grant date:		
Company grants option	No deduction	No deduction
Mary receives option	No tax	No tax
At exercise date (year 5):		
Mary pays $2,000 to exercise options when shares worth $3,000.	Pays no tax (assuming no AMT liability).	Pays tax on difference between exercise price ($2,000) and current FMV ($3,000). $1,000 taxed as ordinary income.
Company receives $2,000 when option is exercised in return for 200 shares.	Receives no deduction	Receives tax deduction of $1,000
At disposition (year 10):		
Mary sells 200 shares for $20/share or $4,000	Taxed as capital gain on difference between exercise price ($2,000) and sale price ($4,000). $2,000 capital gain.	Taxed as capital gain on difference between FMV at exercise ($3,000) and sale price ($4,000). $1,000 capital gain.

Stock option plans are relatively inexpensive to establish and maintain. Legal fees to establish the plan can run as low as $2,000 - $5,000. Administrative costs typically remain low, depending on the complexity of the plan, the number of optionees and whether or not the company is required to register the stock. Unlike some other equity compensation plans (such as ESOPs), stock options do not require independent outside stock valuations. Therefore, the stock price can be determined by a formula, or periodic determination by the Board of Directors, eliminating the need to hire independent experts (see Stock Pricing and Valuation on p. 57). Because an ISO requires that the option price cannot be less than 100% of fair market value at the date of grant, it is critical that your formula reflect fair market value if issuing ISOs to employees.

When to Use an ISO Versus an NSO

The determination to issue NSOs or ISOs to employees should be based on a number of factors including the differences between ordinary and capital gains rates and the potential for corporate profitability and liquidity over the stock option exercise period.

With NSOs, employees must recognize ordinary income when they exercise their stock options based on the difference between the exercise price and the fair market value of the stock at the exercise date. Not only does an ISO allow the employee to defer taxes on the exercise of an option until the stock is sold but it also converts what would be the ordinary income under an NSO to capital gains as long as the employee meets the required holding periods. ISOs therefore become potentially more valuable to employees as the difference between ordinary and capital gains tax rates increase. The drawback for the company is that with an ISO the employer forgoes its tax deduction. However, for companies that do not expect to have taxable income during the period in which the stock options will likely be exercised, it may be more advantageous overall to issue ISOs. This is because the company tax deduction available with NSOs is worth less when the company is not profitable, although deductions may be carried forward to profitable years according to tax laws.

While from an employee point of view, ISOs are usually more advantages than NSOs, it is often more beneficial for the company to grant NSOs. The company will need to weigh the added economic benefit versus the less favorable employee treatment. In fast-growth companies with limited liquidity, when the stock value increases significantly over the option period the employee may not be able to afford to pay the exercise price and the tax on the appreciation due upon exercise of an NSO. There are four ways companies approach the problem of negative employee impact. Some companies are willing to share a portion of the benefits received from their tax deduction with employees by providing a "bonus gross-up" (i.e., a cash bonus that the employee can use to pay taxes upon exercise). This can be more valuable to the employee than the tax savings from an ISO (see "ISO vs. NSO with Bonus Gross-up" on p. 23). In addition, some companies allow employees to pay the exercise price and associated taxes by using current stock that they own, thereby limiting their cash outlay at the time the option is exercised. This is referred to as a stock-for-stock transaction. Public companies generally allow their employees to exercise their options using a "cashless" method, which allows employees to borrow funds from the broker to pay the exercise price, taxes and commissions and immediately thereafter sell shares to pay off the loan.

Companies can also allow employees to deal with this problem by permitting them to exercise their options at the start of the option period, prior to when the stock value has significantly increased. In this case the company would retain the right to repurchase any shares at the exercise price if the employees fail to fully vest in the option.

Finally, the company can simply grant a greater number of NSOs than it would ISOs thereby retaining the company deduction while providing an equivalent after-tax gain opportunity to the employee.

EXAMPLE OF A STOCK-FOR-STOCK TRANSACTION

ASSUMPTIONS:
- Employee A exercises non-qualified stock options worth 100 shares with an exercise price of $10/share when the fair market value at the date of exercise is $20/share.
- Employee A already owns 200 shares of company stock and uses part of the stock to exercise the option and pay applicable taxes.
- Combined federal, state and FICA tax rate is 42%.

Number of Shares to be Exercised	100	(A)
Option Exercise Price	$10/share	(B)
Option Cost (A x B)	$1,000	(C)
Current Stock Price	$20/share	(D)
Number of Shares to be Exchanged (C/D)	50	(E)
Newly Acquired Shares (A - E)	50	(F)
Value of Shares Exercised (A x D)	$2,000	(G)
Option Gain (G - C)	$1,000	(H)
Applicable Tax (H x 42%)	$420	(I)
Stock Sold to Pay Taxes (I/D)	21	(J)
Total Additional Shares Received by Employee (F - J)	29	(K)

The shares exchanged in a stock-for-stock transaction are treated as a "Like Kind" exchange which does not trigger the recognition of capital gains. The shares exchanged carry their original tax basis and acquisition date. Newly acquired shares have a basis equal to the fair market value at the time of exercise. The shares sold to pay taxes represent new shares acquired through the exercise of the option and would therefore not trigger any capital gains.

TAX IMPLICATIONS OF ISO VERSUS NSO WITH BONUS GROSS-UP

ASSUMPTIONS:
- At grant: Mary receives an option to purchase 200 shares at grant price of $10/share (fair market value).
- At exercise: When Mary exercises her 200 shares, the stock has increased to $15/share.
- Tax rates: Combined corporate is 40%. Combined employee is 35%. Capital gains is 20%.

	ISO w/no bonus	NSO w/bonus
Spread at exercise date	$1,000	$1,000
Cash bonus to Mary to pay taxes due	$0	$350*
Corporate tax deduction	$0	$1,350
Tax savings for deduction	$0	$540
Net savings to company (tax savings minus cash bonus)	$0	$190

*While Mary would be required to pay compensation tax of $123 on the cash bonus, with an NSO Mary receives an increase in basis of $1,000 which would reduce her tax liability by $350 when the stock is sold (at $15.00/share).

Advantages and Drawbacks

Advantages

Flexibility of Design: Management can use discretion in determining who receives option awards, how many shares they receive, and whether the shares are subject to vesting, tied to performance objectives, etc.

No Expense on Company Books: Unlike stock bonuses, stock options do not generally require companies to book an expense. Only in the case of a Variable Stock Option (number of shares or exercise price is not known at date of grant) or options issued at less than fair market value is an expense charge required.

Rewards Tied to Company Performance: Because options only become valuable if the stock price increases, they tie employee rewards to future company success. If the company is struggling and the stock price decreases over the option term, the options will not be exercised and thus will not dilute the value to existing shareholders.

Flexible Employee Buy-In: When employees invest their own money to purchase stock it is more meaningful. Stock options require an employee investment, but because the option price is set, employees can plan in advance for the cash outlay required at exercise. In addition, while employees must exercise their options to receive any economic value, the fact that they are not required to do so makes options more attractive to them than stock purchases.

Retention Tool: Most option plans include a vesting schedule requiring the employee to stay with the company for a number of years before they can exercise the full award. This creates a powerful retention tool.

Drawbacks

Difficult to Understand: Due to the complexity of stock options and the tax rules governing them, a comprehensive communications program is required so that employees understand what options mean and how to use them.

Impact on Employee Cash Flow: In most cases, stock options require employees to come up with cash to pay the exercise price. With NSOs, employees must also pay tax on the difference between the exercise price and the fair market value of the stock at the exercise date. This cash outlay can be viewed negatively by employees, particularly in private companies where there may be no immediate opportunity for selling shares. However, because employees can choose to wait to exercise their options, they enjoy great flexibility in determining when to incur this expense.

Options Aren't Equity: Skeptics argue that stock options aren't really equity since no stock actually transfers to employees upon grant, and employees may sell the shares for a gain immediately after exercise. This "churning" of the stock occurs in some public companies where the market provides a ready buyer. In response, some companies give employees an added incentive if they hold the shares for several years after exercise.

Sharing of Control: Upon exercise, employees are entitled to vote their shares, including elections for the Board of Directors. In addition, employee shareholders are entitled to receive information on company financial performance (see Critical Issues on p. 55). Some companies perceive this sharing of control and information as a negative aspect of sharing stock.

Design Considerations

Tie to Business Objectives: Stock option plans should reinforce business objectives. Depending upon a company's goals for the program, options may be awarded to reward past performance, provide incentives for future performance (specific objectives, team performance, market thrusts), match employee stock purchases, recruit key performers, etc.

Length of Option Term: Most options have a 10-year term, although some companies grant options with shorter periods. Because there is a practical limit on the number of options a company can have outstanding, shorter option terms may be conducive to the granting of more options every year. Because longer exercise periods increase the potential value of the option, companies must find the right balance between this value factor and the motivational impact of larger grants.

Vesting: Vesting is usually contingent upon the grantee remaining with the company and thus serves as a retention tool. Vesting can also be tied to the achievement of performance objectives; however, unless alternative vesting at a certain date is assured, this may classify the option as a Variable Option which results in having to book the value of the option as a current expense (see Accounting Considerations on p. 26).

Pricing: Most stock options are granted at the current stock price. This is based on the idea that the reward comes in the future value the employee helps create. A company may discount the exercise price when rewarding employees for past performance. However, any such discount from the current price must be booked as an expense. In the case of a discount, there may be no tax consequence to the employee upon grant, provided there are vesting restrictions and that the discount is not viewed as significant by the IRS. Significant discounts may be treated as a taxable bonus. If the value of the stock has decreased significantly from the exercise price, the stock options are referred to as being "underwater." In certain circumstances, a company may decide to offer to exchange lower priced options for underwater options. Investment groups are generally opposed to repricing for obvious reasons. Still, many companies experiencing sustained stock price pressures feel compelled to reprice to retain key employees.

Annual Awards: Annual stock option awards provide compounded "glue" to help retain employees. Under this approach, at any one time an employee may have several years of options yet to be exercised or vested. In addition, annual awards can have a stronger motivational impact than a single large award.

Size of Awards: The determination of the overall pool of options to make available to employees should be based on a number of factors including the number of employees that will participate in the plan, the employee profiles, the dilution tolerance by current owners and industry practice. The high-tech industry has embraced the use of stock options more than other industries and it has become a competitive requirement for companies in this industry to use stock options to recruit and retain key employees. There is, however, a limit to what shareholders will tolerate regarding the overall pool of options available to employees. This pool is sometimes referred as option "overhang", which is the number of options outstanding or available to be issued as a percent of the total shares outstanding. Most companies have option overhang of less than 10%, although some companies have an overhang as high as 30% or more. In determining how many options to award individual employees, the company must consider if the award will be large enough to be competitive and meaningful to the employee, while being affordable to the employer.

Determining Recipients: A critical consideration in granting stock options is determining who will be eligible to receive the grants. Some companies limit grants to a few key executives, while others spread them more broadly among employees. In determining who should receive option grants, companies should consider how broadly they can make awards while still making sizable enough awards to have the desired motivational impact on the recipients. Many companies have established broad-based option plans where virtually all employees, even international employees, receive option grants.

STOCK OPTION TECHNIQUES

- Merit Stock Options - Stock options granted in lieu of salary increase or bonuses. Short or no vesting schedules are usually attached to these shares.
- Reload Stock Options - The automatic grant of a new stock option when an option is exercised using currently owned stock. Vesting on the reload option is sometimes conditioned upon holding the original option stock.
- Restricted Stock Option - Restricting transfers or sales of stock that is obtained through an option. The post exercise holding period is usually 2-5 years or until termination.
- End of Term Options - The option can only be exercised at the end of its term.
- Performance Based Options - Option vesting schedule based on employee meeting specific performance objectives.
- Indexed Options -The option exercise price increases each year based on a specific index, for example, the consumer price index or the Dow Jones Industrial Average. This requires that the stock price appreciate better than inflation or the average of other stocks before the options have value.
- Transferable Options -Used mainly for senior executives, this technique allows employees to transfer the options to family members prior to exercising them, thereby reducing the overall size of their estate subject to tax.
- Premium Priced Options -The exercise price is set at higher than fair market value at date of grant, requiring the stock to increase a specific amount before the options have value.
- Performance Accelerated Options -Options vest based on time spent with the company. However, the vesting is accelerated if certain performance goals are achieved. These options are still considered fixed options and do not require a charge to earnings for accounting purposes.
- Contingent Options - Options granted if the executive meets specific performance or purchase requirements. These options may be considered variable options and would therefore require a charge to earnings.

ACCOUNTING CONSIDERATIONS

One of the major appeals of stock options is that they are "free" to the company from an income statement perspective. Only when stock options are classified as "variable" or are granted at a price below the current stock price (fair market value) is the company required to recognize a compensation expense for the estimated value of the options. A stock option is classified as variable when the number of shares or exercise price is not known or is contingent upon future events. In the case of an option granted below the market value, the company must recognize a compensation expense equal to the amount of the discount.

In most cases, if the option award is structured properly, the employer is not required to report a compensation expense on its books. However, public companies must use an option-pricing model (such as Black-Scholes) to estimate the impact on net income and earnings per share of the value of the stock options outstanding and disclose in a footnote on its financial statement.

Outstanding options are generally considered to be common stock equivalents, and are therefore factored into certain determinations of earnings per share.

V. 401(k) & Other
Qualified Retirement Plans

One approach to sharing equity with employees using qualified retirement plans is through the use of the popular tax-deferred savings plan known as a 401(k) plan. This type of plan is named for the Internal Revenue Code section which spells out its rules and regulations. In its simplest form, a 401(k) plan is a low-cost method for employers to provide a tax-deferred retirement savings plan for employees. When the plan includes employer contributions of company stock to employee accounts and/or allows employee purchases of company stock, it becomes a method for employees to build equity in the company. A 401(k) plan can also be combined with an Employee Stock Ownership Plan (ESOP) to form what is commonly referred to as a KSOP. KSOPs and 401(k) plans must meet the requirements of both the Internal Revenue Code for qualified plans and the Employee Retirement Income Security Act (ERISA).

How They Work

A typical 401(k) plan permits employees to defer a limited amount of their compensation into any of several diversified investment options established by the plan's administrative committee. The deferred compensation is not subject to current income taxation and any gains on investments are not subject to tax until the assets are distributed to the employee. To encourage employee participation in 401(k) plans, corporate sponsors often match employee contributions with tax deductible corporate contributions of cash or stock.

There are several types of contributions which are typically made to 401(k) plans. The plan may offer any or all of these features:

- *Employee pre-tax contribution*: Employees choose to have the company contribute a portion of their pre-tax salary into the plan account. This type of contribution makes the plan a 401(k). The contribution and increases in its investment value are not subject to income tax until distribution (Social Security, Medicare and, in most states, other payroll taxes are not deferred).
- *Employee after-tax contribution*: Employees may designate an additional portion of their salary, in addition to or in lieu of pre-tax contributions, as a contribution to an after-tax contribution account. Though the contribution is included in annual gross income, increases in its investment value are not subject to tax until distribution.
- *Employer matching contribution*: The employer contributes an amount that matches employee contributions (often according to a pre-set formula) and is sometimes subject to a maximum percentage of an employee's salary or a maximum dollar amount. Matching contributions are often used to encourage lower-paid employees to participate in a 401(k) to help the company meet nondiscrimination requirements and/or to allow higher paid employees to defer a larger portion of their salaries (see Encouraging Employee Participation on pg. 28).
- *Employer non-matching contribution*: Since the host of a 401(k) feature is most often a profit sharing plan, employers may make contributions independent of what employees contribute. These may be tied to profitability and are usually allocated according to salary level. This contribution is often referred to as the profit-sharing contribution of the plan.

● *Qualified non-elective contributions*: In addition, most 401(k) plans provide an opportunity for the company to contribute non-elective salary deferrals (called QNEC's) to force compliance with discrimination tests.

While typically considered savings plans where investments are made in mutual funds or other diversified investments, 401(k) plans may also incorporate a component of equity incentive as well. In the simplest approach, all or a portion of the corporate match of employee contributions may be in the form of corporate stock. If the stock match is applied uniformly as part of the plan design, it is not considered to be an investment decision on the part of employees and therefore generally exempt from securities registration.

In another approach, the plan can be designed to allow employees to invest a portion of their salary deferral in company stock by choice. Companies will generally still offer employees at least three diversified investment options in addition to company stock. In general, a company whose 401(k) plan gives employees the choice of investing in company stock must register with the Securities and Exchange Commission. Public companies have only minimal additional registration requirements, but private companies have to qualify for an exemption from or fulfill federal and state securities regulations. SEC Rule 701, for example, allows smaller companies to avoid securities registration requirements (see details on p. 60).

Because higher-paid employees are usually more interested in deferring a larger portion of their salary than lower-paid employees, 401(k) plans are often structured to encourage greater participation by lower-paid employees to comply with non-discrimination requirements. In addition to requirements applicable to other qualified retirement plans that prohibit "discriminatory" contribution formulas that favor highly paid employees, 401(k) plans must be nondiscriminatory (as defined in Internal Revenue Code Section 401(k)) with respect to actual deferral and actual contribution percentages.

ENCOURAGING EMPLOYEE PARTICIPATION

There are several ways for employers whose 401(k) plans may not meet the IRS discrimination rules to increase participation by lower-paid employees:

● Provide a corporate matching contribution or increase the existing proportion of the match (subject to Internal Revenue Code contribution limits).

● Allow employees to borrow from their 401(k) plans, thereby making these funds available for emergencies or major expenses such as home purchases or financing a child's college education.

● Provide rapid vesting or immediate vesting for employer contributions to the plan.

KSOPs

A KSOP is simply a 401(k) plan which includes and ESOP feature (or vice versa). In its simplest form, an ESOP is combined with a 401(k) plan and the company matches employee 401(k) contributions with a contribution of corporate stock to the employee's ESOP account. As with a standard 401(k) plan, employee contributions are invested in various investment accounts. The company's matching contribution of stock provides an incentive for employees to save for their retirement. A 401(k) with an equity component is sometimes used as a first step towards a special tax-deferred rollover transaction allowed under Section 1042 of the Internal Revenue Code (see ESOPs in chapter VI). The 401(k) would build up ownership over time and then be merged or converted into a new ESOP, which would allow the company to meet the 30 percent ownership requirement for a section 1042 transaction more easily. Such a conversion can trigger federal and state securities issues, however.

Another KSOP strategy for public companies is to pre-fund corporate matches to employee salary deferrals by pre-purchasing or issuing new shares which are then later contributed to the KSOP to meet matching obligations on employee deferrals in the 401(k) plan. Assuming an increasing stock value over time, a corporation can thereby save on the costs of the match and save additional money by taking a tax deduction equal to the value of the future appreciated stock when it is contributed to the ESOP portion of the KSOP. Alternatively, a leveraged ESOP (i.e., one funded through a bank loan) can be used to purchase the shares, allowing employees to benefit from the appreciation in the value of the stock over time. Some companies provide plan participants with current income on their KSOP accounts by passing through the dividend on the ESOP stock to be paid in cash to the plan participants (rather than holding the dividends in the trust). This will generally result in a corresponding tax deduction for the employer based on the Section 404(k) tax deduction rule for ESOP dividends.

IRS regulations require that the ESOP and 401(k) portions of the plan be tested separately for purposes of determining whether the plan discriminates in favor of highly compensated employees. Because anti-discrimination rules are different for 401(k) plans and ESOPs, care must be taken to ensure that both the ESOP and the 401(k) anti-discrimination tests are met.

OTHER QUALIFIED BENEFIT PLANS

Qualified benefit plans such as deferred profit sharing plans and money purchase pension plans typically include stock of companies other than the employer as the primary part of the plan's asset mix. Unlike ESOPs, which are required by law to be primarily invested in employer securities, assets of these plans are generally invested in a diversified portfolio of investments. Because of the fiduciary standards for asset diversification and prohibited transaction rules, it is generally advisable that not more than 30% to 40% of profit sharing plan assets nor more than 10% of money purchase plan assets be invested in company stock, though some profit sharing plans do include a higher percentage.

Profit sharing plans generally, and money purchase plans particularly, are not specifically designed for investment in company stock, though company stock is clearly acceptable as part of the corporate contribution which then becomes part of the asset mix of the plan. ESOPs and KSOPs are specifically designed for investment in company stock and are generally considered more suitable for company stock investments. Except for the employer match on 401(k) salary deferrals which is usually pre-determined, employer contributions to these plans are discretionary. (KSOPs sponsored by private companies usually limit such investments to employer contributions for securities law reasons, though most publicly traded companies offer company stock as a 401(k) employee investment option).

A defined benefit plan or pension plan provides a fixed monthly amount of retirement benefits, usually based on a percentage of salary and length of employment. Most companies fund such plans through an investment trust, no more than 10 percent of the assets of which may be invested in the company's stock. Defined benefit plans rarely invest in company stock for fiduciary and other reasons, though the practice is more common among publicly traded companies. Because these plans are not individual account plans, employees never actually receive the company stock as a benefit, but the performance of the stock can contribute to the overall performance and stability of the plan.

TAX AND COST IMPLICATIONS

Qualified retirement plans such as 401(k)s and KSOPs offer tax incentives to both employers and employees. Subject to maximum contribution limits, all corporate contributions of cash or stock to these plans are fully tax deductible. 401(k) salary deferrals allow employees to defer a portion of their salary to a retirement trust. Contributions made by the employee reduce his or her taxable income while the investment in the trust builds up tax-free until distributed.

Except for special "hardship" situations in 401(k) plans, distributions generally may not be made until the employee terminates employment or attains retirement age (59-1/2 in many plans). However, most plans permit participants to borrow against their 401(k) plan account. If a distribution is made before retirement through termination of employment (or hardship withdrawal, in a 401(k) plan) the employee is subject to ordinary income taxes, and a 10% federal penalty tax may also apply. Some states also have penalty taxes for early withdrawals. However, if the amount is transferred directly to another qualified retirement plan or IRA, taxes will continue to be deferred. In the ESOP portion of a KSOP all the tax incentives afforded to ESOPs are allowed (see ESOPs: Tax & Cost Implications on p. 38). Thus, the KSOP has all the tax benefits of a 401(k) plan and an ESOP.

Because 401(k)s and KSOPs are qualified plans, they are generally more expensive to establish and administer than direct stock purchase, stock bonus, or stock option plans. A basic 401(k) plan without a corporate equity component can usually be set up for somewhere between $1,500 and $8,000. Adding an equity component to the plan can increase the cost of establishing a plan by at least $2,000-$5,000. A non-leveraged KSOP can often cost anywhere between $7,500 and $15,000 to set up, while a leveraged KSOP can cost $50,000 or more depending upon its complexity. Administration, as it is often out-sourced, can add several thousand dollars per year depending on the size and complexity of the plan. Also, these plans, in accordance with Internal Revenue Code and ERISA requirements, typically require an independent appraisal to establish the fair market value of company securities if they are not publicly traded.

If a company is planning to have both a 401(k) and an ESOP, combining the plans to form a KSOP can meet all the objectives of both plans and may reduce administrative costs, since a company's audit, tax preparation, legal and communication requirements are combined in a single plan.

ADVANTAGES AND DRAWBACKS

ADVANTAGES

401(k) plans allow employees to defer federal taxes on compensation and earnings to accumulate tax-free until retirement.

Offers a comprehensive means of providing an opportunity for all employees to participate in employee ownership.

Matching employee contributions with company stock saves the company cash and qualifies for a current tax deduction.

Providing company stock as an investment option allows employees to invest in the company on a pre-tax basis.

Employee investments in company stock can generate capital for the company.

DRAWBACKS

Providing company stock as an investment option raises securities compliance and disclosure requirements and may make it difficult to find a trustee for the plan.

401(k) plans must meet IRS requirements for anti-discrimination. When combined with an ESOP in a KSOP arrangement, the 401(k) and ESOP portions of the plan must be tested separately for anti-discrimination requirements.

For private companies, using company stock in a 401(k) plan of a closely held company requires hiring an independent appraiser to value the stock.

VI. Employee Stock Ownership Plans (ESOPs)

*E*SOPs are tax-qualified, defined contribution plans designed to invest primarily in the stock of sponsoring corporations, thereby enabling employees to obtain stock ownership in their company. As tax-qualified retirement plans, ESOPs are subject to the requirements of the Employee Retirement Income Security Act (ERISA) and to the Internal Revenue Code's anti-discrimination provisions. ESOPs are distinct from other qualified retirement plans in that they are exempt from requirements mandating diversification of investment of plan assets to the extent the ESOP holds qualifying employer securities. In fact, ESOPs are required by law to be invested primarily in the stock of the sponsoring corporation. Their unique ability to borrow money from the sponsoring corporation or a third party lender for the purchase of the sponsoring corporation's stock also makes ESOPs a powerful technique of corporate finance that permits employees to obtain a large equity stake through a single transaction.

How They Work

Non-leveraged ESOPs: A non-leveraged ESOP is similar to a deferred profit-sharing plan in that the company makes contributions to the ESOP trust each year on behalf of its employees. The contribution may be in stock or in cash which can be used to purchase stock or it can remain in cash to diversify the plan's assets. In either case, the corporation receives a tax deduction based on the value of the contribution, subject to Internal Revenue Code limitations. These rules generally limit annual contributions to 15% of payroll for all of a company's qualified plans. In addition, the maximum salary that may be taken into account for purposes of determining contribution limits is $160,000. These contributions are invested primarily in company stock and then allocated to employee accounts based on a pre-determined formula, typically an equal percentage of salary. Employee's accounts grow each year based on company contributions and investment growth on the account balance, and then will be paid out to the employee usually upon retirement or termination of employment.

Leveraged ESOPs: A leveraged ESOP is able to borrow money to purchase employer securities for the benefit of the ESOP participants. While funds can be borrowed directly from the sponsoring corporation, usually a bank or other qualified lender loans money to the ESOP, or, more typically, to the corporate sponsor, which then re-loans the money to the ESOP on substantially similar terms. Stock purchased by the ESOP trust is initially held in a suspense account and allocated to employees as the ESOP loan is repaid. The corporation makes annual (or more frequent) contributions to the ESOP in an amount at least equal to the ESOP's debt repayment obligation to the lender. Annual corporate contribution limits are increased to 25% of payroll for purposes of repaying the principal on leveraged ESOP debt, plus unlimited interest and "reasonable" dividends which are also tax deductible under section 404(k) of the Internal Revenue Code. As the ESOP loan is repaid, an equivalent portion of the unallocated shares is released from the suspense account and allocated to employee accounts according to a pre-established written formula, usually based on salary, though other non-discriminatory formulas may be used. Because corporate contributions to an ESOP are tax deductible within certain limitations, both the principal and the interest payments on ESOP loans are generally fully tax deductible to the sponsoring corporation.

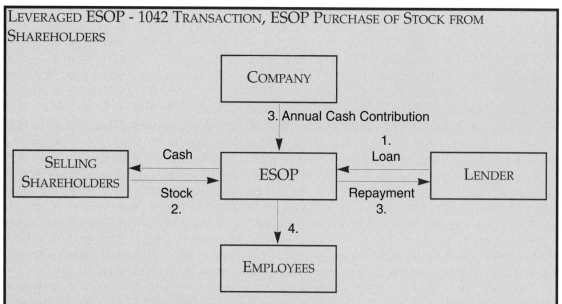

LEVERAGED ESOP - 1042 TRANSACTION, ESOP PURCHASE OF STOCK FROM SHAREHOLDERS

1. Lender lends money to ESOP with company guarantee.
2. ESOP buys stock from existing shareholders, who reinvest proceeds in "qualified replacement property." (The tax deferred Section 1042 transaction is not permissible in Sub-S Corporations.)
3. Company makes annual tax deductible contributions to ESOP which in turn are used to repay lender.
4. As the loan is repaid, shares are allocated to employee accounts based on a pre-set formula. Employees receive a distribution when they retire or leave the company.

More typically, the lender will make the loan directly to the company which then makes a "mirror loan" on substantially similar terms to the ESOP. The net corporate tax impact is identical in either scenario.

Employees generally become eligible to receive the vested portion of their account upon the occurrence of certain events such as job termination, retirement, death or disability. For companies whose stock is not publicly traded, the corporation must provide the employees with a put option on shares distributed to them when they leave the ESOP. This put option obligates the corporation to repurchase the shares within a specified 60-day period in the year following distribution or during a similar period in the next succeeding year. The put option lapses if it is not exercised by the participant during either of these two periods. The corporation must repurchase the shares. The corporation may, however, extend to the ESOP the option to repurchase the shares subject to the put option. If the ESOP accepts this obligation, it may then use cash in the trust to purchase the shares. Payments for the repurchased shares may be deferred for pre-retirees and spread over several years.

Employees who terminate service prior to attaining retirement age must begin to receive their ESOP distribution within five years after the end of the plan year in which they terminated. In addition, the company can spread those payments over five years in equal annual installments, with reasonable interest paid on the unpaid amounts. Employees who have attained retirement age must begin to receive their ESOP benefits within one year after the end of the plan year in which they retire. Again, the company may defer payments over five years in equal annual installments. Companies may choose to accelerate ESOP distribution schedules but all employees must be treated equally and once a distribution schedule has been established, the corporation may not amend the plan's rules to the detriment of employees' interests. Most closely-held companies therefore adopt a conservative distribution schedule.

ESOP distribution rules require that employees be given the right to receive the shares in their ESOP accounts. ESOP distributions from public company ESOPs are typically made in lump-sum distributions of shares since employees can simply sell their shares on the stock market. As noted above, most closely-held firms tend to repurchase the shares over time. In addition, closely-held companies that are "substantially employee-owned," which is generally interpreted to mean that the company is owned at least 80% by current employees, may require departing ESOP participants to accept cash payments in lieu of their ESOP stock. This provision allows employee-owned companies to preserve their employee-owned status over time. In actual practice, however, departing employees almost always prefer to receive cash distributions from the ESOP.

In order to protect ESOP participants from undue investment risk as they approach retirement age, Congress passed a law in 1986 requiring ESOP participants to be provided with diversification options. Under the ESOP diversification rules, employees with 10 years of participation in the ESOP and who have attained the age of 55 must be given the option of diversifying up to 25% of the shares in their ESOP account. The option must be made available to eligible employees during a 60-day period during the year in which they become eligible, and the option must be made available to the employee on the same terms each year through age 59. When the employees attain age 60, they must then be given a one-time option to diversify up to 50% of the stock in their accounts. To meet the diversification option, employers must provide at least three alternative investment options within the ESOP or another qualified employee benefit plan (typically a 401(k) plan) or the employer can choose to make a cash distribution to the employee of the diversified amount. If such a cash distribution is rolled over into an IRA, it is not considered to be an early distribution from the plan and is therefore exempt from early withdrawal taxes.

> *With certain exceptions, ESOPs must satisfy the Internal Revenue Code's requirements applicable to defined contribution plans. Critical issues that should be addressed in plan design include determining:*
>
> - who will participate in the plan
> - how the stock will be allocated to participants
> - what vesting schedule will be used
> - whether shares will be voted by a trustee or passed through to the participants
> - how distributions of ESOP accounts will be handled
> - whether or not to use preferred stock for the ESOP
> - the rights and preferences (if any) of the ESOP stock
> - the extent to which corporate financial information will be provided to plan participants

Federal law requires that an ESOP pay no more than fair market value for shares it acquires. The creation of an ESOP in a privately held company requires an independent appraisal to determine the fair market value of the stock at least on an annual basis and for all significant transactions involving the ESOP.

Because of the put option, closely held ESOP companies are required to provide a market for shares distributed to employees. To prepare for this "repurchase liability," a financial plan should be developed to ensure sufficient liquidity for repurchasing the ESOP stock from departing employees. Companies may plan for and meet their ESOP repurchase liability in a variety of ways, including making substantial cash contributions on an annual basis and acquiring corporate owned life insurance (COLI) to cover the plan's liabilities.

INNOVATIVE APPROACHES

ESOPs as an Exit Strategy

For owners of closely held C-Corporations, one of the most attractive features of ESOPs is the ability to defer capital gains taxes on sales of stock to an ESOP when certain conditions are met. Established under Section 1042 of the Internal Revenue Code and commonly referred to as the "ESOP Rollover," this provision of the law not only provides an attractive incentive for shareholders of closely held businesses to sell their shares to an ESOP - in other words, to the employees - but also offers a potential solution to the often difficult problems of shareholder liquidity, management succession and transition to second generation ownership.

A retiring owner, or any major shareholder of a privately held company who wishes to sell his or her stock, faces some potentially unwelcome choices. Often the seller is forced to choose between selling to outside investors, if any are available; exchanging stock with another company in a merger; or selling stock back to the company, if such a transaction is feasible. None of these options is taxed as favorably or gives the selling shareholder diversification options as a sale to an ESOP. And, unlike a sale to an ESOP, the other choices may result in unwanted consequences for the company's independent existence and the jobs of employees.

An ESOP rollover sale offers tax-advantaged terms to the selling shareholders, establishes a potential market for future sales of stock, helps maintain current employees' jobs and rewards employees with an ownership stake. At the same time, it helps retain independence and local ownership of the business. A sale to an ESOP also allows an owner to sell out gradually, withdrawing from the business to whatever extent desired.

Under section 1042, a shareholder or a group of shareholders acting in a single transaction who sells qualified securities to an ESOP incurs no taxable gain on the sale if three principal conditions are met:

First, the stock sold must be securities of a closely held company that have been purchased for full fair market value and the shareholder must have owned the qualified securities for at least three years. Qualified securities do not include stock acquired through stock options or qualified retirement plans.

Second, immediately after the sale, the ESOP must hold at least 30% of each class of outstanding stock of the corporation or 30% of the total value of all classes of outstanding stock, including options issued by the corporation. Once the ESOP obtains a 30% stake, all subsequent sales to the ESOP may also qualify for the tax deferral as long as the ESOP maintains at least a 30% stake.

Third, within a fifteen month period beginning three months prior to the date of sale, the seller(s) must purchase qualified replacement property (stocks or bonds of U.S. operating companies), execute a written statement of election at the time of purchase and file those statements with the IRS with that year's tax return. If the cost of the replacement property is less than the amount derived from the sale of securities to the ESOP, the difference is currently taxable. Proceeds from the sale to the ESOP that are invested in qualified replacement property are sheltered from capital gains taxes until the replacement property itself is subsequently sold. (If the selling shareholder dies before the replacement property is sold, the capital gains taxes will usually be avoided altogether.) The cost basis of the shares sold to the ESOP carries over to the replacement property.

Stringent regulations apply to tax-deferred ESOP sales. For example, family members, direct lineal descendants of the selling shareholder and other 25% shareholders may not receive allocations on any of the stock for which a seller chose the 1042 deferral. In addition, many lenders require the selling shareholder to pledge part or all of the replacement property as security for the ESOP loan. But, if carefully structured, this provision offers entrepreneurs an excellent exit strategy on tax-favored terms while also providing employees with an opportunity to obtain substantial equity in their company.

FINANCIAL BENEFITS OF AN ESOP LOAN WITH A 1042 INVESTMENT ROLLOVER

Assume a 100% ESOP buyout from a private seller with a transaction value of $10 million and a negligible or zero tax basis in the securities sold.

SELLER BENEFITS

Section 1042 of the Internal Revenue Code enables shareholders of privately held C-Corporations who have owned their shares for at least three years to reinvest the proceeds from a sale of stock to an ESOP into U.S. domestic corporate securities (either public or private) on a tax-deferred basis if the sale results in the ESOP owning at least 30% of the company stock.

1042 ROLLOVER BENEFIT COMPARISON	NON-ESOP	ESOP
Gain on sale	$10,000,000	$10,000,000
Tax (combined federal and state capital gains of 26%)	2,600,000	0*
Net Proceeds	$ 7,400,000	$10,000,000

REINVESTMENT BENEFIT

Additional After-Tax Proceeds on 1042 sale	$2,600,000
After-Tax Reinvestment Return (assumed)	.07
Annual Income Stream Increase ($182,000 x 15 years)	$2,730,000
(life expectancy 15 years -- cumulative benefit)	

Total Benefits Produced from Tax Savings (15 years)	$5,330,000

* If replacement property passed to seller's estate, no taxes will be paid on the transaction.

COMPANY BENEFITS

Deductible principal and interest payments over the life of the ESOP debt. Because principal and interest payments on ESOP debt are tax deductible, the pretax cash flow required to service the principal of ESOP debt is reduced.

	NON-ESOP	ESOP
Pretax earnings required to service debt:	$16,666,667	$10,000,000
Combined federal and state tax (@ 40%)	$ 6,666,667	$ 0
After-tax earnings available for debt service over the life of the ESOP loan	$10,000,000	$10,000,000

FACILITATE CORPORATE DIVESTITURES

Another common use of leveraged ESOPs is to facilitate corporate divestitures of divisions by using the ESOP to purchase a significant number of shares on behalf of the employees in the divested company. In this approach the parent corporation will typically pay the legal and financial costs associated with the ESOP loan and will sometimes either provide a guarantee for the ESOP loan and/or retain some equity in the divested company. To reduce ESOP loan costs, employees will frequently be given the option of investing other defined contribution plan assets such as profit sharing or 401(k) benefits into the new ESOP. Lenders usually require the management team to invest additional funds outside of the ESOP in exchange for potentially higher equity rewards if the ESOP loan payments are made on time. More rarely, this same approach can be used to structure an ESOP leveraged buyout in which an ESOP loan is used to purchase all or most of the shares of a public company in order to take the company private.

FINANCE INVESTMENTS OR ACQUISITIONS

ESOPs can also be used to finance investments or acquisitions by having the ESOP purchase newly issued shares. If the sponsoring corporation simply issues new shares and contributes them to the ESOP, the amount that may be contributed is limited to 15% of covered payroll. It is possible, however, for the corporation to structure a leveraged ESOP loan, backed by a corporate guarantee, to acquire a large block of newly issued shares. The proceeds from that loan can then be used for any legitimate corporate purchase such as acquisitions or capital investments. As the ESOP loan is repaid, the ESOP participants capture the benefit of that newly created value as the ESOP shares are allocated to their individual accounts.

USE OF PREFERRED STOCK

Federal law requires that ESOPs must own the best common stock in the company (ESOPs may not, for example, own non-voting shares). Some companies use a strategy of structuring a convertible preferred stock for the ESOP. The use of convertible preferred shares offers several advantages. The primary purpose of this strategy is to make efficient use of the Section 404(k) tax deduction for dividends declared on ESOP stock. The higher dividend rates typically paid to preferred stockholders allow a company to pay down ESOP debt more rapidly through the use of deductible dividends without having to make the same dividend payments on the company's common stock. Once the ESOP loan is repaid, the ESOP can provide employees, through dividends, with current cash income from their ESOP accounts on the same tax deductible basis. ESOP convertible preferred shares are sometimes used in KSOP arrangements as well, whereby dividends on convertible preferred shares purchased or acquired through a corporate match in the employee's 401(k) account are used to provide employees with current income on their savings. An added advantage is that convertible preferred shares carry additional liquidation rights, thereby providing greater security for the ESOP participants.

TAX AND COST IMPLICATIONS

ESOPs offer a number of tax advantages to the corporate sponsor, selling shareholders and employees. Subject to Internal Revenue Code limitations, all corporate contributions to ESOPs are tax deductible. As a result, payments made to repay ESOP debt result in a tax deduction within Internal Revenue Code limits for both principal and interest payments on the loan. In addition, limits on deductible contributions to qualified plans are increased from 15% to 25% of covered payroll for contributions to leveraged ESOPs. For C-corporations, interest and "reasonable" dividends applied to repay ESOP debt are not subject to the 25%-of-payroll limitation. While dividends paid to stockholders are not normally deductible by the paying corporation, section 404(k) of the Internal Revenue Code provides that dividends declared on ESOP shares which are paid in cash to plan participants or applied to the repay-

ESOPs AND S CORPORATIONS

Effective January 1, 1998, a corporation electing to be treated as an "S corporation" for federal income tax purposes is able to sponsor an ESOP. Previously, employee benefit trusts were not permitted as shareholders of an S corporation.

In an S corporation, the shareholders, not the corporation itself, are subject to tax on the corporation's income, whether it is distributed to them as dividends or retained in the corporation. The Taxpayer Relief Act of 1997 provides that an ESOP trust in an S corporation will be treated as a single shareholder, rather than counting each participant in the plan as a shareholder. In addition, the ESOP is exempt from the unrelated business income tax (UBIT) that applies to other employee benefit trusts in Federal S corporations. S corporation ESOPs may also require ESOP participants to take their ESOP benefits in cash rather than in stock in order to preserve the company's S corporation status.

S corporation ESOPs do not, however, qualify for some of the ESOP tax advantages available to C-corporations. Individual shareholders of S corporations do not qualify for the Section 1042 tax-deferred sale; the increased contribution limits for leveraged ESOPs are not available to S corporation ESOPs; and ESOP dividends are not tax-deductible in S corporations.

Nevertheless, the fact that S corporation ESOPs are exempt from the Federal UBIT liability offers potentially significant tax savings to many companies. S corporations are not subject to tax at the corporate level and, though the income will be passed through to its individual shareholders, no shareholder-level tax will be imposed on the ESOP because it is a tax-exempt entity. In effect, the income tax will be deferred until the participants in the ESOP receive their benefit distributions. On the other hand, for S corporations with non-ESOP shareholders, those shareholders must generally withdraw sufficient funds to cover payment of their taxes on the corporation's income. If tax distributions are required to be made to the shareholders other than the ESOP, an equivalent distribution must also be made to the ESOP because the economic rights of the ESOP's shares must mirror the rights of the other shareholders. This may result in an increased drain on the corporation's cash flow.

ment of leveraged ESOP debt are tax deductible to the corporate sponsor. However, the deduction received for dividends paid may subject the company to corporate alternative minimum tax. In addition, dividends used for ESOP debt repayments must be "reasonable."

ESOPs may be relatively expensive to set up compared to other equity-based plans. Legal fees typically range from $7,000 to $20,000 for non-leveraged plans, and can be much higher for complex transactions. The legal requirements for an independent appraisal will add to the annual costs as will the costs of plan administration if such expertise is not available in-house. Leveraged transactions add additional complexities. Feasibility study costs, trustee fees, bank fees and legal and investment banking expenses vary widely, depending upon the size and complexity of the transaction. Leveraged ESOPs for small companies typically cost more than non-leveraged ESOPs, sometimes running hundreds of thousands of dollars for larger, more complex transactions. Companies who carefully study and implement well planned ESOP strategies can receive tax benefits greatly in excess of these costs.

SUMMARY OF TAX INCENTIVES OF ESOPS

Employer contributions of stock or cash are tax-deductible (within applicable limits) and are tax-free to participants until distribution. Contribution deduction limits have been increased from 15% to 25% of payroll for ESOP debt repayments. In C-corporations, interest and "reasonable" dividends used for ESOP debt repayments are not subject to the 25% contribution limit.

Income is exempt from federal and state taxes while held in the ESOP trust. (Some states may tax income in Sub-S ESOPs.)

Income-averaging and 'rollover' provisions minimize the tax on distributions.

Capital gains taxes may be deferred on sales of stock to an ESOP in a closely held C-corporation if, after the transaction is completed, the ESOP owns at least 30% of company stock and sale proceeds are reinvested in qualifying securities of domestic corporations.

Terms of purchase may be highly leveraged by the ESOP borrowing funds to purchase most of the stock.

Both interest and principal repayments are tax-deductible on leveraged ESOP debt.

Cash dividends on ESOP shares are generally deductible in C-corporations if passed along to participants or if used to repay an ESOP loan taken out to finance the purchase of company stock.

ESOPs in S corporations are exempted from the UBIT tax.

ADVANTAGES AND DRAWBACKS

ADVANTAGES

Provides benefits of stock ownership to all full-time employees. Does not require a change of management control to accomplish this.

Has unique ability to borrow money to purchase employer securities to facilitate a variety of corporate finance and ownership transition objectives.

Enables employees to acquire a large block of stock paid for over time through the future earnings of the corporation rather than from their own savings.

Offers significant tax advantages to the company, employees and selling shareholders.

Enables transfer of ownership to management and employees rather than an outside party for business succession or other changes in corporate control.

DRAWBACKS

Stock allocations must be made according to a pre-established formula which is normally based on gross income, including bonus payments.

Independent appraisal of stock value is required annually for private companies.

Implementation costs, legal and administrative fees may be more expensive than most other equity compensation plans, especially with a leveraged ESOP.

Must meet stringent anti-discrimination rules spelled out by the Internal Revenue Code.

Employees aged 55-60 with 10 years of participation in the ESOP must be given an opportunity to diversify a portion of their stock holdings in the plan.

Financial obligation of put option for private companies. This "repurchase liability" can be substantial for successful companies that realize significant appreciation in the value of their stock. ESOPs in sub S corporations may acquire substantial cash dividends which can be used to fund a portion of "repurchase liability."

Accounting treatment for leveraged ESOPs can have negative implications for publicly traded companies.

ACCOUNTING CONSIDERATIONS

According to AICPA Statement of Position 76-3, Leveraged ESOP debt must be recorded on the balance sheet of the corporate sponsor as a liability. The offsetting entry is a reduction in equity (contra equity account). This negative accounting treatment makes large leveraged ESOPs problematic for public companies. Shares held in the suspense account are not treated as outstanding for the purpose of calculating earnings per share.

VII. Alternative Forms of Equity Compensation

Non-Qualified Deferred Compensation Arrangements

*I*n recent years, the maximum compensation that may be taken into account by qualified retirement plans has been reduced and the maximum individual income tax rate has increased. In response, there has been increased interest in non-qualified deferred compensation arrangements by executives and their employers.

Non-qualified deferred compensation arrangements are traditionally used to defer taxes and build wealth for key executives. Such arrangements avoid many of the complex and administratively burdensome requirements that govern qualified plans under ERISA and the Internal Revenue Code. In addition, they can be tailored with great flexibility to fit precise objectives and be targeted for specific employees or groups of employees. Because of this flexibility, and the ability to incorporate company stock into the plan, non-qualified plans make ideal tools to attract, retain, and motivate key employees.

How They Work

Deferred compensation arrangements fundamentally consist of an agreement between an employer and an employee that payments due for current services will be made at a future date. The employee's tax objective is to ensure that taxation does not occur until payments are actually received, while the employer's tax objective is to ensure that it receives a full deduction at the same time. The built-up value of investment income may also be tax-deferred to the individual. Specific tax issues arise depending on the type of funding arrangement.

Non-qualified deferred compensation arrangements vary widely because each is tailored to the specific needs of the company and specific key employees. However, the common features of such plans are that they are designed to supplement the salary and/or bonus compensation that employees may defer above various statutory limitations for qualified plans. In some cases the company offers a guaranteed investment return to encourage employees to defer their salary. One innovative approach is to use these arrangements with an equity component to tie employees to company performance over the long term on a tax-deferred basis.

One type of plan, called an excess benefit plan, is designed to supplement the contribution limitations of Internal Revenue Code Section 415, which limits employer and employee pre-tax total contributions to qualified retirement plans to the lesser of $30,000 (with regulatory cost-of-living adjustments) or 25% of an employee's taxable income. Excess benefit plans are partially or completely exempt from ERISA, depending on funding arrangements.

A top-hat plan (sometimes referred to as a Supplemental Executive Retirement Plan or SERP) provides deferred compensation to a select group of management or highly compensated employees. In order to qualify as a top-hat plan, a plan must be both "unfunded" and benefit a select group of management or highly compensated employees. It is vital that the employees included in a top-hat plan be limited not only in number, so that the plan will be select, but also in rank.

Top-hat plans are exempt from the participation, vesting, funding and fiduciary requirements of ERISA, but are subject to limited reporting and disclosure requirements. The most significant of these reporting requirements is that the employer must file a brief, one-time disclosure statement within 120 days of plan inception and be prepared to provide plan documents upon request.

FUNDING STRATEGIES

A popular strategy for funding deferred compensation plans is called a Rabbi Trust. The earliest IRS approval of this was a private letter ruling involving deferred compensation provided by a congregation to its rabbi, hence, the term "Rabbi Trust." A Rabbi Trust is an irrevocable trust in which assets are set aside for the exclusive use of satisfying an employer's contractual obligation to pay deferred compensation. It can be funded in any manner including cash, insurance products or company stock (see Using Equity in Deferred Compensation Arrangements on p. 45). Rabbi Trust assets are subject to the claims of general creditors but are inaccessible to the company for discretionary use until benefit obligations are met.

The Rabbi Trust has now become the norm in most current deferred compensation planning. Early Treasury Department regulations in the income tax area provided that a taxable transfer occurs when assets are set aside in trust or escrow "beyond the reach of the employer's creditors." This suggests that assets that are set aside, but not beyond the reach of the employer's creditors, would not be taxable.

This concept was established by a long series of private letter rulings by the IRS, followed in 1992 by a model Rabbi Trust intended to be used as a safe harbor. In practice, the model trust has become more of a requirement rather than a safe harbor because the IRS has announced that it will not issue rulings on any unfunded deferred compensation arrangements that use a trust other than the model trust, except in rare and unusual circumstances. In addition, the Department of Labor has ruled on several occasions that a top-hat plan supported by a Rabbi Trust is unfunded for purposes of Title I of ERISA.

In order for employees to reap the tax-postponement rewards of deferred compensation plans while preserving the compensation tax deduction for the employer, top-hat plans and most excess benefit plans must be carefully structured to be recognized as "unfunded" by the IRS. To be considered "unfunded," plan assets must remain unsecured and may not unconditionally vest in, or be transferable by, the employee beneficiary. Any "unfunded" plan must clearly provide that participants have the status of general unsecured creditors. There are several common strategies utilized to fund these plans.

Under a corporate-owned life insurance (COLI) plan, the company pays insurance premiums on cash value life insurance policies for plan beneficiaries. The policy initially provides only a death benefit to the employee's estate, but when the employee's deferred compensation becomes payable, the company can use the built-up cash value of the life policy to fund the obligation. As with other top-hat funding methods, COLI assets are still subject to creditor claims, so such arrangements provide no benefit security in the event of bankruptcy. Moreover, the policy value cannot be linked to the value of the compensation benefit, so at the time of payout the company may have either invested more than necessary in policy premiums or not enough to cover benefit obligations.

A third-party guarantee whereby a surety bond or letter of credit provides that the guarantor — a bank, surety or insurance company — will indemnify a covered employee if the employer defaults on its obligation to pay deferred benefits is another common strategy. These devices may provide security while they are in effect, but coverage is expensive, rarely obtainable for more than a few years, and their purchase may subject the employee to unfavorable tax treatment.

Another way to provide and secure retirement benefits outside of a qualified retirement plan is through a non-qualified annuity. The executive who is vested in the annuity contract is subject upon purchase to current taxation on the premium amount, but will not pay tax on the inside buildup until payout. The cash surrender value of an annuity is subject to immediate taxation, but an annuity contract with low or zero cash surrender value can provide the employee with benefit security while incurring little or no present tax liability.

USING EQUITY IN DEFERRED COMPENSATION ARRANGEMENTS

- Employer grants stock to employee or employee defers salary to purchase stock
- Stock is contributed to a Rabbi Trust
- Employee's deferred account grows with the value of the stock
- Vesting can occur over seven years, or longer if employee is considered "top-hat"
- Distributions can be made in cash or stock
- Employee defers all income taxes until distribution. Employer receives a corresponding deduction at the time of distribution
- Employer records an expense based on the value of the award spread over the vesting period

TAX AND ERISA ANALYSIS

There are two critical danger areas that must be analyzed with regard to non-qualified deferred compensation plans. The first is the extent to which the plan is subject to ERISA. The second is income taxes.

ERISA applies to any employer-sponsored program that provides retirement benefits or that defers income until termination of employment or later. There are, however, a few narrow exceptions. At the time of deferral, the employee must elect when to receive distribution from the plan. If it is a top-hat or excess benefit plan, the senior executive may defer distribution until retirement. If employees who do not qualify under the definition of "top-hat" participate in the plan, they must be paid out over a shorter period expected to end before retirement. Taxes must be paid at the time of distribution.

In determining whether a non-qualified deferred compensation plan succeeds in deferring taxation to the date of its actual receipt, two general tax principles must be considered. The Economic Benefit Doctrine sets forth that the promise to pay deferred compensation, in order to avoid taxation, must be "subject to substantial risk of forfeiture," e.g., not beyond the reach of the employer's creditors. In addition, the Doctrine of Constructive Receipt refers to how the compensation is set aside for the employee, including the use of trust mechanisms. As a result of IRS pronouncements on the income tax consequences of non-qualified deferred compensation plans, various guidelines have been established to help ensure that a plan will not become an audit target, although many of these do not have the force of the law.

The costs of implementing a non-qualified deferred compensation plan may be as low as $3,000 depending upon plan complexity. They are typically administered in-house. If a Rabbi Trust is used, there are additional costs associated with establishing the trust.

GUIDELINES FOR PRESERVING TAX DEFERRAL

Following these guidelines will help ensure that a plan will be recognized by the IRS as "unfunded" in order to take advantage of favorable tax treatment:

- The deferred amount must not be unconditionally placed in trust or escrow for the benefit of the employee
- The promise to pay the deferred amount must be a mere contractual obligation of the employer, not evidenced by notes or secured in any way
- The election to defer must be made before the beginning of the period of service for which the compensation is payable, unless the plan imposes a substantial forfeiture provision that remains in effect throughout the entire period of deferral
- The plan must define the time and method for payment for each event that entitles a participant to receive benefits
- The plan must state clearly that participants have the status of general unsecured creditors of the company and that the plan constitutes a mere promise to make payments in the future
- The plan must specifically prohibit the transfer or alienation of a participant's interest
- The plan must state that it is the intention of the parties that the arrangement be unfunded for tax purposes and for purposes of Title I of ERISA
- If the plan uses a trust, the trust must take the form of the model Rabbi Trust described in Revenue Procedure 92-64 except in rare and unusual circumstances. Employers should always request a letter ruling from the IRS regarding any proposed rabbi trust

Advantages and Drawbacks

Advantages

Non-qualified deferred compensation plans are highly flexible and can be designed to suit any number of specific individual and corporate objectives.

"Non-discrimination" restrictions do not apply to non-qualified plans; employers have great latitude in creating plans for key employees.

Income in excess of the maximum compensation limitations for qualified plans ($160,000 in 1998) may be deferred in non-qualified plans.

Accumulated investment value (i.e., the initial deferral and earnings) is not subject to taxation until the compensation is paid.

Drawbacks

Plans must be limited to a select group of employees and therefore are not suitable for broad-based equity sharing.

Plan assets are subject to the claims of the employer's creditors in event of company insolvency or bankruptcy. An employee has no rights to the assets other than as a general unsecured creditor.

Deferred compensation accounts must be charged as a current expense on the company's books.

Rabbi Trusts must be established based on a model set forth by the IRS or by obtaining a private letter ruling. Rabbi Trusts are not operative under the laws of some states.

The cash value of Corporate Owned Life Insurance policies (COLIs) is difficult to accurately project into the distant future, so current set-asides may be too much or too little to cover actual payout obligations.

Accounting Considerations

Deferred compensation must be expensed on the company's books in the year the compensation is deferred if it is 100% vested when deferred. If a vesting schedule is used, the expense would be booked over the vesting period. As the account is credited with earnings, an additional expense is recorded. This can result in significant current compensation expense. The company would book a corresponding liability based on the value of the account.

When company stock is used in a Rabbi Trust, the company is only required to book an expense and liability based on the value of the stock at the time of grant. Additional increases in the value of stock would not be booked as an expense.

INTERNATIONAL EQUITY COMPENSATION PLANS

In recent years a growing number of multi-national corporations have begun to share stock ownership with their international employees. Some of these companies seek to replicate the success of their U.S.-based plans in motivating employees to think and act like owners and to provide a common incentive and equitable treatment to their U.S. and non-U.S. employees. Other companies seek to use stock ownership to help establish a common international identity for the corporation among its widespread workforce and to keep more of its stock in friendly hands. Another motivation is simply to provide international employees with U.S.-denominated securities which can often be an attractive benefit for employees, especially in developing economies.

International equity plans can take several forms. One common approach is to issue stock options. Some companies make a one-time grant of a set number of options to each employee. Others provide employees with options equal in value to a given percentage of pay each year or provide option awards for selected employees based on individual merits. Often the companies provide international employees with a 24-hour loan facility whereby they can direct a designated stock broker in the United States to give them a loan sufficient to exercise their options. The broker then immediately sells enough shares to pay off the loan and transaction fees and deposits the remaining shares in the employee's account.

Another approach to international equity plans is to create an "International ESOP" in a tax-free haven. Each of the company's international subsidiaries are given an account within the trust and each participating employee has an individual account with the appropriate subsidiary. The subsidiary corporations then either purchase shares of the parent corporation based on profitability or receive grants of stock from the parent and those shares are allocated to the accounts of the participating employees. The shares are held in trust for the employees; at termination of service, the ESOP trustee sells the employee's shares and makes a distribution of the proceeds to the employee. This has the advantage of alleviating securities registration concerns in most countries as well as avoiding certain country regulations associated with the ownership of shares in foreign corporations.

Some companies have successfully implemented stock purchase plans similar to Section 423 or Section 401(k) plans, though the plan rules need to be modified to conform with local laws. In these plans the plan custodian typically collects employee salary deferrals and makes periodic purchases of the company's stock on behalf of the employees.

Another common approach is to provide restricted stock grants to key executives. The shares are held in trust on behalf of the employee until the restrictions lapse, at which time the employee can either receive the shares or request that the trustee sell the shares and distribute the sale proceeds to the employee.

In establishing an international equity plan, corporations need to recognize that separate securities laws apply in each country where employees will participate in the plan. In most cases, securities registration is required, though the process is not usually as expensive or time-consuming as in the U.S. In addition, local rules apply to the taxation of employee benefits and plan administrators must be prepared to keep the plan distribution rules in conformity with local norms. In some cases, currency exchange controls and employment laws may be an important consideration in determining how employees will acquire their shares. For example, in some countries, a corporate grant of stock as a benefit may be deemed to be a "regular and recurring benefit" which may not be taken away from the employee or may be subject to special severance or other retirement benefit calculations. Collective bargaining rules can be an issue in other jurisdictions.

Due to the complexities of international equity plans, the costs for such plans, including securities registration, recordkeeping, custodial and legal fees, can be high. The sponsoring company must be prepared to deal with tax, accounting and securities issues on a country-by-country basis, no matter which type of plan it may choose. However, the benefits of a common incentive, motivation and shared identity among multi-national employees in an increasingly global economy can be an attractive reason for establishing an international equity plan, and growing numbers of employers are using stock incentives as a key strategy to motivate and reward their international employees.

IMPORTANT CONSIDERATIONS

In considering the establishment of an international equity participation plan, corporations need to consider a number of important issues:

- Securities laws - Securities registration is usually required. Some countries' laws prohibit the ownership of shares in foreign corporations. An alternative approach in these jurisdictions is to provide employees with phantom shares.

- Plan administration - Careful coordination with the stock plan administrators in each foreign subsidiary is necessary in order to process employee purchases and make allocations to the appropriate accounts. Currency conversion issues are frequently a key administrative concern.

- Taxation - Differing tax laws may make administration of a centrally managed plan difficult and require careful monitoring of changing tax law requirements.

- Communications - Language and cultural barriers should be given careful consideration in order to minimize difficulties.

VIII. Simulated Equity Methods

Simulated equity methods are specialized deferred compensation and incentive compensation tools designed to provide employees with the economic benefits of stock ownership without the employee having to purchase stock or the corporation having to transfer actual ownership of stock. Other factors relevant to the consideration of simulated equity methods compared to actual stock ownership include securities registration requirements, accounting and tax treatment, and the flexibility to tie stock value to a specific aspect of the company's business. Two of the most common types of simulated equity methods are Stock Appreciation Rights and Phantom Stock arrangements.

How They Work

Stock Appreciation Rights: Stock Appreciation Rights (SARs) are the right to receive the appreciation value (the spread between the market price and grant price) of a certain number of shares of company stock over a specific period of time in cash, company stock or some combination of the two. SAR plans can be combined with stock option plans having the same vesting and exercise dates to give the employee a choice of either paying cash for shares of stock or receiving the cash value of the stock appreciation. Some plans provide that the exercise of SARs or stock options is mutually exclusive; others allow employees to exercise a combination.

SARs were commonly granted to corporate officers subject to the insider trading restrictions of Section 16(b) of the Securities Exchange Act of 1934. SARs allowed them to obtain the equity in their options without a simultaneous purchase and sale of the option shares. However, changes in Rule 16b-3 in 1991 removed the simultaneous purchase and sale problem for options. Exercises of in-the-money options are no longer treated as a purchase under 16(b). Also, changes in Federal Reserve regulations now permit broker-assisted "cashless exercises" of options, which eliminates another need once filled by SARs. Because of these regulatory changes, and because of the adverse accounting treatment of SARs, their use has diminished significantly, particularly in public companies. A growing number of private companies, however, see SARs and phantom stock as an attractive means of providing stock-based incentive awards without diluting actual stock ownership.

Market value is the most common method for valuation of stock appreciation rights, but value may also be linked to corporate earnings, book value, a percentage of profits, a percentage of operating cash flow above a return threshold, a percentage of economic value added (a measure of economic returns above the cost of capital) or the performance of a business operating unit if its value can be accurately determined.

Phantom Stock: Phantom stock represents units of value that correspond to an equivalent number of shares of stock granted to an employee for a specific period of time. Upon maturity, the employee is compensated, in cash or stock equivalent, in an amount based on the increased value of the phantom stock. Phantom stock plans can include dividends, which can be either paid currently or accrued for payout when the phantom shares mature. Unlike most stock appreciation rights, phantom stock arrangements typically have a fixed award date.

TAX AND COST IMPLICATIONS

If structured properly, there are generally no tax consequences upon grant of a SAR or phantom stock. Tax is generally deferred until exercise or maturity, except for SARs that are linked to stock options. If the SAR is exercised for cash, the company receives a corresponding deduction as a compensation expense; if it is exercised for stock, the company may deduct, as a business expense, the amount of income recognized by the employee.

Any amounts received by an employee or set aside and made available to the employee, whether in the form of cash, stock, or otherwise, are taxed as ordinary income and the company is entitled to an equivalent compensation deduction. No income is recognized for phantom dividends while they accrue, only when they are paid or payable in cash.

Both SARs and phantom stock represent a future cash liability to the company equivalent to the appreciation value of SARs or the full value of phantom stock shares, respectively.

INNOVATIVE APPROACHES

SARs can be used to make up for the loss of share value of options when the stock price has declined or not risen above the exercise price.

Because SARs or phantom stock do not necessarily have to be tied to the value of the company's shares, they permit flexible design of a long-term incentive program. For example, they can be tied to increases in sales, increases in return on investment or the performance of a particular subsidiary or division.

Another use which is becoming more common is linking voluntary deferred compensation plans with a phantom stock feature. Executives who defer salaries or bonuses under an unfunded deferred compensation plan may elect to have the value of their deferred benefits measured by the value of company shares in a phantom stock approach.

Phantom shares can be used to provide a retirement program for key employees in which the company determines the amount of contributions as a basis for growth in fund value over a specific period of time, with the actual contribution subject to financial performance. The contributions are then invested in phantom shares, with the ultimate value of the deferred funds tied to phantom share value.

A portion of annual bonus payments can be invested in phantom shares as a means of emulating the practice of many public companies that requires senior executives to meet individual ownership guidelines through an "at-risk" investment in company stock.

Phantom stock or SARs may also be used by U.S. multinationals to provide the economic equivalent of stock options or restricted stock grants to employees of foreign subsidiaries or branches where local tax, securities or exchange control rules make use of stock unfeasible.

EQUITY COMPENSATION IN LIMITED LIABILITY CORPORATIONS (LLCs)

Most states have now passed legislation authorizing Limited Liability Corporations (LLC) as an approved form of corporate ownership. In an LLC, ownership of the corporation's assets may be shared with employees. However, those shared interests are not actually in shares of stock, but ownership units.

The distinction is important in considering ownership sharing arrangements with employees in LLCs. For example, LLC s may not grant incentive stock options (ISOs) since ISOs are defined by the law as options on shares of stock. Similarly, LLCs may not establish ESOPs since ESOPs must by law own the issuing corporation's best common stock. LLCs may establish the equivalent of stock purchase plans using hybrid forms of equity similar to phantom stock or stock appreciation rights (SARs).

Employee owners in Limited Liability Corporations are liable for taxation on their allocable share of the company's income, even if the distribution is not received. LLCs typically make a distribution to the owners to cover the tax liability and the owners get a step up in the basis of their ownership rights. Bookkeeping issues may become difficult if the LLC's ownership changes frequently during the year, since profit or loss must be allocated among all individuals who were owners at any time during the year and the company's books must be closed and computations made at the time of each change in ownership. Allocation of tax liability can also be made by prorating a full year's results based on the number of days during the year that each individual was an owner.

ADVANTAGES AND DRAWBACKS

ADVANTAGES

Stock appreciation rights and phantom stock plans furnish a way to provide employees with the long-term motivational benefits of stock appreciation and tie employee rewards to shareholder gains without diluting the ownership rights of existing shareholders.

Avoid issues concerning minority shareholders (where that is a concern).

Long vesting and exercise periods coupled with multiple awards over time in either type of plan can serve as a performance-based retention tool.

Both types of plans are highly flexible and adaptable to a variety of objectives.

The plan is self-funding in that payments are deferred until performance results actually create the economic value required for the award payment.

The plans can be structured so that employees may not have to purchase shares or exercise stock options, both of which require a cash outlay.

For companies that are not publicly traded, establishing formulas for SARs and phantom stock can avoid the complexity and expense of hiring an independent valuation firm.

Plans can be structured to reward performance based on the economic value added to divisions or subsidiaries where it is possible to separately measure that performance.

Not having to actually issue shares of stock avoids administrative and regulatory complexities, a particularly useful consideration for foreign corporations or their U.S. subsidiaries for whom issuing stock to U.S. employees may be impossible or impractical.

DRAWBACKS

For accounting purposes, the company must book the value of outstanding SARs or phantom shares, plus accrued dividend rights, if any, as a compensation expense against income in the year of the grant and then adjust the entry each year as the value of the "stock" increases or decreases.

Both types of plans represent a potentially significant cash drain on the company when an employee's cash entitlement matures.

Employees have no actual equity ownership unless the award is paid in stock.

If the entitlement is in the form of stock, securities registration requirements may apply.

Lump sum awards may create a significant tax liability and the award is taxed at normal tax rates rather than at capital gains rates.

ACCOUNTING CONSIDERATIONS

The value of SARs and phantom stock, plus appreciation and/or dividends in subsequent years, is treated as a compensation expense and charged against earnings in the year of the grant or vesting, and is normally prorated to the number of years after which the employee is entitled to receive the compensation. Variations in the value of outstanding SARs or phantom stock rights require periodic adjustments to company earnings to reflect the potential compensation expense and liability.

IX. Critical issues

$\mathcal{T}$here are a number of critical issues that entrepreneurs, owners and managers must understand and address before implementing an equity-based compensation plan. By understanding these issues up front, companies can take the necessary steps to structure their programs properly to avoid problems that could arise later.

Dilution of Ownership and Control

The decision to share equity with employees is often quite different from a decision to establish other benefit and profit sharing arrangements. Ownership goes to the heart of participation in private enterprise. Both the current owners and top managers of a corporation contemplating some form of employee stock ownership need to be prepared psychologically, organizationally and financially for a change in the ownership dynamics of the organization. For an equity compensation plan to be effective, support and commitment from the top of the company is essential. Top managers need to be willing to promote the concept of employee ownership aggressively in order for the plan to have the desired impact on employee attitudes and, ultimately, on corporate performance. Broad-based equity sharing requires a different style of leadership, and thus managers must be willing to listen to employees' concerns, share information with them and involve them in improving their work processes and environment.

Of equal importance is the readiness of current owners to share equity and thereby give up absolute or partial control of the enterprise. Issues concerning stock voting rights, financial disclosure and control of the corporation are often stumbling blocks for owners of private businesses who aren't always comfortable with the idea of sharing ownership and information with other shareholders, even those within their organization. Yet the most effective employee-owned organizations find a way to create an environment in which shared information and employee participation help foster more effective organizational relationships based on the shared risks, rewards and responsibilities of ownership. When equity incentives are designed effectively to fuel growth, productivity and profitability, the dilution to existing shareholders results in them benefiting from a "smaller piece of a bigger pie."

Voting:

In using direct ownership methods such as stock purchase plans, stock bonuses or stock issued upon exercise of stock options, the employer must, as with all shareholders, allow employee shareholders to vote their shares on all matters that require a shareholder vote, including election of the Board of Directors. The company generally cannot control these votes through a trustee or other mechanisms. In some cases it may be possible to use non-voting stock, but management must balance its objectives of wanting employees to act like owners against not giving employees all the rights that go with ownership.

There are various ways to address unwanted dilution impacts. Non-voting shares can be used in some instances to mitigate the dilution of voting control or, in the case of qualified plans in non-public companies, voting of the shares (for most issues) can be controlled by the trustee of the plan, which can be an insider of the company. In some plans, such as ESOPs, employees must be given pass-through voting rights on major corporate issues such as mergers, acquisitions and sale of substantially all of the company's assets. Some corporations pass through voting of the shares in these plans to the employees, allowing them to provide direction to the trustee on the voting of the shares in their accounts. This can reinforce the feeling of ownership among the employees. In public companies, voting rights on allocated shares must be passed through to ESOP participants on all issues. However, the Department of Labor and IRS require the trustee in all cases to vote the shares in the best financial interests of plan participants.

Voting rules for shareholders are governed by a company's charter and by the state where it is incorporated. Each state has different rules regarding voting, although shareholders generally vote on the following issues:

- Election or removal of the Board of Directors
- Adoption or amendment of the company's bylaws
- Merger or consolidation of the corporation with another company
- Transfer of substantially all of the property (assets) of the company
- Voluntary dissolution of the company
- Required additional capital investments by shareholders to the company
- Substantial change in corporate structure

Dilution:

It is important for owners to distinguish the difference between percentage dilution and economic dilution. Depending on the type of equity strategy a company chooses, shareholders may have to incur either percentage and/or economic dilution. The important issue is to fully understand all of the ownership and economic impacts of the plan. Often entrepreneurs express concern when their percentage ownership decreases, when in reality the economic value of their ownership often increases. Stock ownership should be shared with employees with the intention that the added incentive it provides will yield a greater overall company value and thus a greater value for all shareholders than if no stock was shared.

In determining the amount of dilution you can accept, it is often useful to develop a "Dilution Model" under different growth assumptions that can show you how much dilution you can accept and still have a satisfactory return on your shares.

EXAMPLE OF A DILUTION MODEL

ASSUMPTIONS:

- Over a 4-year period employees receive a total of 250,000 shares of stock.
- Company value increases 20% per year.

Dilution Model

At Start of Plan:	Value of Company	$2,000,000
	Founder's Shares	1,000,000
	Employees' Shares	0
	Price Per Share	$ 2.00
	Founder's Percent of Ownership	100%
	Founder's Value of Ownership	$2,000,000
After Year 4:	Value of Company	$4,150,000
	Founder's Shares	1,000,000
	Employees' Shares	250,000
	Price Per Share	$ 3.32
	Founder's Percent of Ownership	80%
	Founder's Value of Ownership	$3,320,000
	Employees' Percent of Ownership	20%
	Employees' Value of Ownership	$ 830,000

In this example, the Founder's ownership percentage decreased from 100% to 80%, while the economic value of ownership increased from $2,000,000 to $3,320,000.

Financial disclosure:

Financial disclosure is another concern of many business owners. Shareholder rights to receive information differ for companies whose securities are registered with the SEC versus privately held companies.

Publicly traded companies must periodically disclose financial information to their stockholders. For a private company, the state in which it is incorporated and the registration or exemption requirements for the particular plan you are using will determine the amount of information that must be given to employee shareholders. The laws of many states do not give shareholders the right to receive regular financial information.

In regard to a private corporation, the company needs to consider these minimum standards in light of the desired goal to have employees improve corporate performance. Without knowing and understanding some measures of financial performance, employees will have little ability to judge the impact of their efforts on overall corporate performance. To provide employees with the ability to measure the effectiveness of their efforts, at a minimum, sales and profitability figures should be communicated to employees including, if possible, further breakdowns of income and costs by business division.

With regard to qualified plans, federal regulations require that employees receive a summary plan description and annual statements as to the value of their personal account in the plan and the value of the share price of employer securities within the plan. In using direct stock ownership methods such as stock purchase plans, stock bonus plans and stock option plans, the employer must provide full and fair disclosure of all material information about the company to employee shareholders.

STOCK PRICING AND VALUATION

One of the most critical issues associated with equity compensation in closely held companies is the valuation of employer securities. Companies whose shares are not traded on an established market generally must adopt a procedure for providing employee shareholders with a value for their shares. In the early growth stage of the company, the company usually has a low valuation which is hard to measure. Because of this difficulty, share value is commonly determined using a formula price for the shares as a proxy for fair market value. As companies grow or their transactions become significant, companies will likely find it beneficial to ensure that stock transactions are made at fair market value. An independent valuation firm can help a company determine its fair market value, which incorporates qualitative and quantitative factors affecting the company and the performance of comparable firms, the public stock market, and the economy in general.

For Employee Stock Ownership Plans (ESOPs), federal law requires that the shares of closely held corporations be valued at least annually by an independent valuation firm. For other qualified retirement plans such as 401(k) or profit sharing plans, an independent appraisal is not an absolute legal requirement, but is strongly suggested, particularly if the plan is involved in a transaction that results in a significant transfer of ownership. There are different approaches that an independent appraiser may take in determining fair market value. The most accurate and widely accepted methods take into consideration current market conditions, company specific issues relating to historical, current and projected corporate performance (both quantitative and qualitative issues) and the performance of comparable public companies in similar or related fields.

One of the most critical issues is making sure employees understand how the shares will be valued when the shares are ultimately repurchased by the company. Most equity compensation plans in private companies provide that the Board of Directors, using good faith and fair judgment, will determine the fair market value of company stock. In many cases, the Board will hire an independent valuation firm to help them make the determination.

STOCK PRICE FORMULAS

There are a variety of approaches companies use for establishing a value for stock transactions. Historically, many companies have used book value or a multiple of book value. This approach can be useful in start-up companies where there is little intrinsic value and key employees can obtain a significant number of shares at a low price. However, using book value has limitations: it is potentially volatile; is of questionable validity for companies with few tangible assets other than the employees themselves; and lacks any direct reflection of outside market conditions. A more sophisticated approach to stock pricing formulas tries to incorporate a variety of factors both in terms of internal measures of corporate performance and external market conditions. Provided below are two examples of formulas that incorporate a variety of internal and external factors. Note that even these sophisticated formulas still rely, at least occasionally, on the opinion of independent valuation experts to ensure that the formulas reflect fair market value.

1. The following formula is used by one company to value its shares quarterly for the purpose of establishing a share price for conducting trades and selling and repurchasing shares among employees and plans. This formula takes into account current shareholders' equity and net income for the prior four quarters. It does not take into account projected earnings.

The 5.66 multiplier is a constant that was used when the formula price was first established. The market factor was originally established at a value of "1" and is adjusted up or down based on the performance of comparable publicly traded companies, the overall stock market, industry outlook and the economy in general. Because the company's stock plans include an ESOP, federal law requires that an independent appraiser provide an opinion whether the formula price reflects fair market value.

$$E/W1 + 5.66MP/W$$

E = Stockholders' equity

W1 = Common stock and "equivalents" outstanding at end of quarter

M = A "market factor" set by the Board of Directors and reviewed by an independent valuation firm to assure that the formula price reflects "fair market value"

P = Net income for previous four quarters

W = Weighted average number of common stock and "equivalents" for the previous four quarters

2. This stock valuation formula is used by a company whose stock compensation program relies heavily on the use of stock options. This formula includes many elements of the formula in the first example but also includes projections of the next 12 months' earnings. The company brings in an outside appraiser every few years to determine whether the formula price represents fair market value.

$$\frac{SE + SN + CX + 7FG}{SI + SV}$$

SE = Stockholders' Equity

SN = Subordinated Notes

CX = Cost to Exercise Vested Options

SI =   Shares Issued and Outstanding

SV =   Vested Stock Options

FG = $\dfrac{\text{Last 12 Months Gross Earnings + Projected Gross Earnings Next 12 Months}}{\text{Past 24 Months Gross Earnings}}$

SECURITIES REGISTRATION

Stock compensation in the form of bonuses, direct compensation, or as contributions to employee benefit plans generally are not considered to be a sale of securities and therefore would not fall within the scope of federal securities registration requirements. The use of stock options or stock purchase plans is generally considered an offer for sale and would fall within the scope of federal securities registration requirements. State securities laws differ significantly from federal law and from one state to the next. It is therefore advisable to have any stock compensation plan reviewed by an attorney to ensure conformity with federal and state securities laws.

All securities offered for sale by a company must be registered with the Securities and Exchange Commission (SEC) and with a state regulatory authority unless the company qualifies for an exemption from federal and/or state securities registration requirements. In addition, companies are required to file periodic reports with the SEC if they have securities listed on a national exchange or have more than 500 shareholders and $5 million in assets. The Securities Act of 1933 and the Securities and Exchange Act of 1934 spell out these rules. Compliance with them can be time consuming and very expensive. Significant exemptions apply, so before issuing shares to employees, it is critical for a company to determine if its offering falls within one of the securities registration exemptions. Otherwise, significant expenses will be incurred if shares must be registered.

State securities laws, sometimes called Blue Sky Laws, often differ significantly from each other and federal securities laws. In some cases, Blue Sky Laws impose even stricter standards than federal securities laws, so care must be taken to research the applicable securities laws in every state in which a company seeks to offer or sell stock.

On the federal level, there are several possible securities registration exemptions for closely held companies. Whether a company qualifies for a specific exemption generally depends on how many and what types of people will purchase shares, how much money will be raised from the sale of securities, and how much information will be given to the investors. Some of the potential federal securities registration exemptions include:

1. Most companies are not generally required to register stock sales with the SEC if less than $1 million is raised from the related issuance of shares within a one-year period.

2. If a company raises between $1 million and $5 million from related issuance over a one-year period, it can generally sell stock without SEC registration to an unlimited number of accredited investors and up to 35 non-accredited investors. Accredited investors are directors, executive officers and others whose individual net worth exceeds $1 million or whose annual income exceeds $200,000 for the previous two years and is expected to exceed $200,000 in the current year. Information requirements under SEC rules for this exemption will consist of general information on the company and its operations.

3. If a company raises over $5 million from related issuance over a one year period, it can generally sell stock without SEC registration to up to 35 investors and an unlimited number of accredited investors. More detailed information on the company and its operations must also be furnished as a requirement of this exemption.

4. As noted above, stock granted to employees through certain tax-qualified benefit plans such as ESOPs, 401(k) and profit sharing plans are generally exempt from federal securities registration requirements to the extent that employee contributions are not used to purchase the stock. Even stock given as compensation is not considered to be a sale of securities (provided the employees could not elect to receive cash or other property) and is therefore exempt from federal securities registration requirements in most cases.

5. SEC Rule 701 provides a limited exemption for securities sold pursuant to written compensatory benefit plans or agreements. This exemption is particularly attractive for small, closely held corporations interested in offering their stock under options, or in a 401(k) or Section 423 discount purchase plan.

6. There may be a federal exemption for stock sold by a company having all of its investors resident in the same state in which it conducts most of its business operations. Sometimes referred to as the "coffee shop rule," this exemption requires careful planning and strict execution.

It is important to remember that even if the sale of shares may be exempt from federal registration requirements, all issuance of securities must be registered or issued under an exemption from registration in each state in which the company or any of its investors is located. The transfer of shares must also meet all federal and state anti-fraud rules which require fair and full disclosure of all material information about the issuing company.

SEC RULE 701

The Securities and Exchange Commission (SEC) adopted Rule 701 to provide an exemption for securities registration requirements for offers and sales of securities pursuant to certain compensatory benefit plans and contracts relating to compensation.

Under Rule 701, stock may be offered for sale to a company's employees, directors, general partners, trustees, officers or consultants pursuant to a written compensatory benefit plan. The aggregate amount of stock that may be sold in a single offering under this exemption is subject to several limitations. Not more than a)$500,000, b)15% of the total assets of the employer or, c)15% of the outstanding securities of the employer may be sold in any individual offering and, in addition, the total shares offered may not exceed $5 million in any 12-month period. Stock offered under Rule 701 must also be a single discrete offering not subject to integration with any other stock offering, and such stock is deemed to be restricted securities subject to resale limitations.

Though stock issued under Rule 701 is exempt from federal securities registration requirements, the rule does not exempt issuers from the anti-fraud rules and the requirements to provide fair and full financial disclosure to employees or other persons within the scope of the rule, nor does it provide exemptions from state securities registration requirements.

STOCK RESTRICTIONS

Subject to state corporate and securities laws prohibiting unreasonable restraints on the sale of securities, companies may attach almost any type of restrictions to their shares. While the corporation cannot place an outright prohibition on an employee selling his or her shares, certain closely held companies can use restrictions to control the conditions under which the shares are sold to avoid the problem of shares falling into the hands of competitors or other persons having interests adverse to the corporation. When determining which restrictions to implement, it is important for the company to find an acceptable balance between the advantage of restrictions that maintain control over the shares versus the potential disadvantage of the restrictions diminishing the attractiveness of the stock as a motivator for employee shareholders.

Two important stock restrictions that many closely held companies attach to their shares are the right of repurchase at termination and the right of first refusal. The right of repurchase at termination gives companies the right, but not the obligation, to purchase shares from employees who terminate employment with the company. Generally, this right must be exercised at the current fair market value of the shares, although the shareholder agreement can specify a pre-determined repurchase value. The right of first refusal gives the company the right, but not the obligation, to match any legitimate offer for the shares from outside interests. These restrictions are usually incorporated in shareholder agreements, or in the company's charter or bylaws.

Stock Restrictions

Right of First Refusal: Controls who owns stock by allowing company to match any purchase offers.

Right of Repurchase at Termination: Keeps company employee-owned by allowing company to purchase stock from terminating employees.

In many cases, companies attach a vesting schedule to stock options and to stock purchases. Vesting schedules usually require the employee to stay with the company over a set number of years before he or she can exercise or keep the total number of shares upon termination. Vesting may also be tied to meeting specific performance objectives although you should check with your accountants because this type of vesting may require a charge to your earnings for accounting purposes. Annual stock awards with multi-year vesting schedules can be an excellent tool for employee retention because employees may have several years' worth of awards unvested at favorable prices.

Other common restrictions relate to the time period before an employee may sell securities received in a stock award. Examples of these restrictions include "career restricted stock" in which shares are forfeited if the employee leaves the company prior to retirement; "career shares" in which shares received as payment of compensation cannot be sold as long as the employee remains with the company; and "deposit shares" which are a specified amount of stock an employee must own and hold in order to receive subsequent stock awards. These types of restrictions are typically reserved for key employees as a means of having them own significant amounts of stock over a long period of time, therefore tying their long-term compensation more directly to overall corporate performance.

It is especially important for S corporations to include stock restrictions that give the company the right to approve any transfers of stock, thereby protecting the company's S corporation status.

However, it should be stressed that state securities laws and regulations may limit the type of restrictions that a company can attach to its shares.

Liquidity

Regardless of the type of equity sharing plan a company uses, if the company is closely held it has a practical and moral and, in some cases, legal obligation to create liquidity for employee shareholders at some point. Optimally a company will provide some mechanism by which employees can sell at least some of their shares while they are still employed by the company. If insufficient liquidity is available for a timely repurchase of shares, that factor will be taken into account by independent valuation firms who may then discount the value of the stock. In addition, the lack of liquidity can decrease the value and motivation of employee ownership. Companies must therefore plan carefully for their liquidity needs in order to have sufficient cash flow to repurchase employee shares and to support the value of the shares of current stockholders.

For stock ownership to ultimately benefit the shareholder, there must be a market for the shares. For closely held companies that do not plan to go public, this obligation is most often borne by the corporation itself. There are various ways for a company to provide liquidity. The most straightforward method of creating shareholder liquidity is simply an unscheduled purchase of shares by the corporation as cash flow permits. As cash flow becomes more predictable, it may be possible to establish a regular schedule of stock repurchases according to a set program. To provide more predictability to the process, many companies agree to repurchase shares upon termination of employment. These repurchase agreements typically include a provision allowing payments to be spread over a number of years with a market rate of interest on the value of the unpurchased shares. Each program provides various levels of liquidity at different stages of the company's development.

One way to mitigate the need for corporate repurchase of shares while allowing employees to receive cash from some of their stock holdings without having to leave the company is to establish an internal stock market. Several companies have begun to establish such mechanisms, though the applicability of this concept generally requires that corporations have a relatively large number of shareholders and be willing and able to undertake the expense of registering their securities.

Federal law provides ESOP participants with a "put option" that requires the corporate sponsor to repurchase ESOP shares from employees at fair market value when they leave the company or retire. In many cases, the company will direct the ESOP to repurchase the shares using cash built up within the plan. This legal obligation or "repurchase liability" can be deferred through plan design, which governs vesting and distribution rules. In many cases corporations purchase corporate owned life insurance (COLI) to help finance their repurchase liability.

COMMUNICATIONS AND INFORMATION SHARING

Employee ownership creates the financial incentive for employees to work harder and smarter. But it takes more than just a financial incentive. Employees must understand how the business runs and how their performance impacts the company.

Ownership can have multiple meanings, and employee stock ownership in a corporate environment touches on a wide range of issues including compensation, corporate governance, sharing of financial information, employee empowerment and labor-management relations. Furthermore, many employees have had little or no exposure to stock ownership prior to its introduction in a corporate setting. In establishing equity sharing programs, corporate managers need to be sensitive to the differing expectations and assumptions that employees may have and should therefore place great importance on communicating the overall philosophy of the equity sharing program with employees. Clear and effective communications is one of the essential elements of effective employee ownership programs; its importance is often underestimated by corporate managers.

At a very basic level, plan sponsors have a legal obligation in qualified plans to provide participants with a summary plan description, annual updates showing the value of the assets held in their individual accounts, and any amendments made to the plan document. Beyond these basic minimums, however, lies the challenge of getting employees to think and act like owners in such a way as to help improve corporate performance.

X. Making Ownership Real

$\mathcal{T}$he most challenging aspect of making employee ownership work effectively over the long-term is getting employees to think and act like owners. Volumes have been written on this and related topics. Approaches are as numerous and varied as the companies that employ them. Here we will touch on some of the key issues related to developing an ownership culture that companies should consider as they implement their equity compensation program.

A company in which employees think and act like owners creates the potential for numerous synergies to enhance corporate performance. The company benefits by having employees treat customers with extra care, look for opportunities to create efficiencies in how they do their jobs and use their creative energies to take on responsibilities to enhance productivity and competitiveness. The employees benefit by working in an environment that challenges them, values their opinions and ideas, and rewards them with a piece of the action. The shareholders, including employees, benefit by enjoying the increased returns that this innovative, efficient organization creates.

On the other hand, giving employees stock ownership, without opportunities to participate in bettering the company and access to information on company performance, can evoke cynicism from employees and create morale problems.

The ingredients of a true "ownership culture" include both tangible and intangible elements. The tangibles are tools such as newsletters for communications, organizational structures to enhance employee participation and skills development programs for education and training. The intangibles stem largely from the founders or managers of the company and their core values — their leadership style, the vision they set and inspire others to believe in and the environment they set for trust and communications. In the most successful organizations, the tangibles and intangibles complement and reinforce one another. For example, a flat organizational structure can reinforce an environment of open communications among employees of all levels. Similarly, a rigid, hierarchical organizational structure can make even the best of management's efforts to encourage open communications fruitless. Another potential for contradiction occurs when the leaders do not embody the values they espouse. The role of the intangibles in defining a corporate culture cannot be underestimated.

So how do companies achieve an environment that is mutually beneficial for the corporation and its employees at the same time? There are four important elements:

Information Sharing, so that employee owners are knowledgeable about the company, its performance, their working environment and how they will participate in stock ownership.

Education and Training, so that employee owners understand what drives company performance and have the skills to participate in improving it.

Employee Involvement, so that employee owners can be heard on a wide range of issues from workplace redesign to marketing strategies and even corporate governance.

Meaningful Financial Participation, in which the potential financial benefits of ownership can have a sufficient impact on an employees capital accumulation to serve as a real incentive.

INFORMATION SHARING

Regardless of the media used to communicate with employees, the most important factor in communications is that it be authentic. Even when the news is somewhat negative - for example, if an equity program is being implemented along with salary reductions to cut costs - it is better to be up-front with employees about the situation than to candy-coat the message. Most employees can see through to the truth, and if they can't, the grapevine will tell them.

In terms of the types of information to communicate, employees first of all need information on the equity compensation plan itself. Why did the company do it? What is it meant to accomplish? How will the plan work? Very simply, how do the employees gain equity in the company? Do they have to achieve certain performance goals? Will managers make recommendations? Will all employees receive an equal percentage based on salary or some other formula? The risk of not communicating this information effectively is that employees may perceive the program as a ploy by management to enrich themselves or perhaps reduce employee benefits.

It is also important for senior management to communicate with employees about company initiatives, such as new contract wins, new market thrusts, policy and benefits changes and organizational restructuring. Employee owners need to be informed in order to understand the nature of the company and its plan for success. Regarding the sharing of financial performance, the fact is that many employees, regardless of their level in the company, do not understand financial statements. There are a number of examples of companies that have gone beyond the legal requirements for financial disclosure and provide frequent and easy-to-understand financial information along with an explanation of the trends, abnormalities and problem areas so employees can understand the meaning behind the numbers. Employees with a basic understanding of the "corporate scorecard" are in a better position to understand the impact of their actions on corporate performance. In a larger company, it helps to provide employees with information on their division or business unit's performance as well, and how that contributes to the big picture. Employees are most concerned about their own work environment and need to know how their work affects the overall company. It is critical to keep people informed of the financials, the stock price and how their performance is connected to those measures.

EMPLOYEE EDUCATION AND TRAINING

Optimally, employee education and training will include some aspect of mentoring and career development, skills cross-training and business education, all of which assume a certain amount of flexibility and empowerment for employees as compared to traditionally managed firms. Skills cross-training enables people to appreciate another person's job and how their performance affects that person. Some companies provide financial skills training to all employees so they can read the company's financial statements and understand what is happening. Employee education and training also signifies an investment in the work force, which sends an important signal to employees that management recognizes the value of investing in employee education and has made a commitment to them.

EMPLOYEE INVOLVEMENT

Employee involvement occurs in both formal and informal ways in an organization. Some companies have formal structures such as committees or teams for employees to participate in improving company operations. An important factor is the degree to which employees in these groups are empowered to make decisions relating to improved company performance and customer service. Some companies foster more informal methods of employee participation such as an open-door policy and a casual environment where anyone can talk to anyone and offer suggestions, regardless of the chain-of-command. Many companies have committees to address work environment issues, although some recent National Labor Relations Board rulings affect the level to which employee committees can be involved in benefits and other work place decisions. Some companies organize task forces to tackle strategic problems and encourage employees of all levels to participate. Frequently, employees are appointed or elected to serve as representatives on committees overseeing the management of equity plan assets. Some companies have an employee representative on the Board of Directors, giving employees involvement at the highest level of corporate governance. Other companies allow an employee representative to attend Board meetings and other management meetings and report back to employees.

MEANINGFUL FINANCIAL PARTICIPATION

For employee ownership to have a positive effect on employee attitudes, motivation and productivity, corporate sponsors need to invest sufficient amounts in the ownership program so that an individual employee's ownership stake can become meaningful over time. There is no simple guideline for what is "meaningful," particularly when the ultimate value of stock ownership will depend upon the performance of the company itself. Nor is it a function of the overall percentage of a company owned by the employees. A 1% stake in a large and profitable company may be more valuable than a 25% stake in a small, struggling firm.

Ultimately, employees will judge the benefits of employee ownership by what it means to them personally. A small or insignificant amount of financial benefit through ownership is not likely to have a strong impact on an employee's attitude or behavior. On the other hand, a company with prospects for substantial stock appreciation can justifiably limit current stock compensation in lieu of potential long-term benefits for the employees.

The benefits a company provides through ownership need to be considered in light of salary, benefits and other incentive-based compensation. Each company will need to implement its ownership strategy accordingly, but several general principles have been used by companies in which ownership is intended to provide a meaningful incentive.

- Consider ownership as a percentage of an employee's annual compensation. A goal may be to provide employees with a certain percentage -- for example 50-100% of their annual compensation in the form of stock ownership within a certain period of time, say four to five years.

- Measure the value of ownership as a percentage of annual compensation. Annual stock compensation in excess of 5% of salary plus appreciation is generally considered to be sufficient as to have a meaningful impact on an employee's net worth.

These examples have to be considered in light of the type of stock compensation plans a company implements and its long-term ownership strategy. Ultimately, employee ownership from an employee's perspective must include the potential financial benefits that an ownership stake can provide.

Investing in these core elements and providing employees an important opportunity to affect the life of the organization can make ownership a powerful organizing theme. Not only does ownership tie employees directly into the wealth creating capacity of the corporation, it also conveys a broad range of rights and responsibilities. The right to information and voting rights on corporate governance issues are counterbalanced by the responsibility to protect and enhance the investment in the company.

In conclusion, the Foundation has found that employee stock ownership works best when the following characteristics are present:

- The leader articulates a clear vision for sharing equity.
- Equity sharing is designed to logically (and fairly) support the company goals and culture.
- Emphasis is placed on communications – about the company, the stock plan, the company's vision and mission and the corporate culture.
- Liquidity is provided within a reasonable time frame.
- Employees are treated like owners by being given responsibility, autonomy and opportunities to offer feedback and ideas.
- Equity participation is meaningful, not token.
- All employees are given the opportunity to own stock.
- The company is committed to growth.

Equity incentives, when designed to be an integral part of a company's culture and reward system, are powerful tools for reaching the hearts and minds of employees. The challenge lies in creatively structuring equity incentives to have the greatest desired effect on the company and employees.

APPENDIX: SUMMARY OF RESEARCH

$\mathcal{T}$he following tables are reprinted by permission of Douglas Kruse and Joseph Blasi, from their article in Handbook of Human resources, copyright JAI Press, 1996.

TABLE 1: Employee Satisfaction Under Employee Ownership

Authors of the studies	Source of data	Explanatory variables	Main results
Comparisons between employee-owners and non-owners			
1. Greenberg 1980	Surveys of 550 employees in 4 U.S. plywood cooperatives and large non-employee-owned firm	Co-op membership	Higher work satisfaction for co-op members, and greater participation in cooperative functions associated with higher satisfaction.
2. Hammer, Stern, and Gurdon 1982	Surveys of 233 employees in 2 firms saved by employee buyouts, 1-2 years after buyouts, 1976-77	Ownership status Ownership stake	Ownership stake not linked to satisfaction; satisfaction similar for owners and non-owners in one firm, while higher for owners in other firm (but no difference for prdn. workers in later survey) Lower alienation from work among owners in both firms.
3. Long 1978b, 1980	Survey of 87 employees 6 mos. after 70% bought trucking co., and at knitting mill w/30% owners	Ownership status	Higher satisfaction for owners, but due to perceived participation rather than simple ownership status
4. Kruse 1984	Surveys of 325 employees in two ESOP cos., 1981, compared to 548 employees in national random sample	ESOP membership	ESOP members had similar satisfaction to national sample in retail company, lower satisfaction in manufacturing company, the latter due in part to bitter strike one year before study.
5. Russell et al. 1979	Surveys of 165 employee-owners in 6 U.S. refuse collecting firms, compared to 541 non-owners, 1977	Ownership status	Owners had similar satisfaction levels as comparable non-owning employees, but were more likely to say they would take the same job again
Pre/post comparisons			
6. Long 1982	Three surveys of 147, 184, and 248 employees, first one prior to employee purchase of Canadian	Employee buyout after first survey Ownership stake	Satisfaction up for those perceiving increased participation, but down for those perceiving no change in participation. No relation to ownership stake.
7. Tucker et al. 1989	Two surveys of 38 and 39 employees at fast-growing small U.S. firm, 1982-84	ESOP adoption after first survey	Satisfaction up (but sample too small for significant results)
Comparisons within groups of employee-owners			
8. Buchko 1993	Survey of 218 employees in an ESOP company, 1987	ESOP account value Perceived influence from ESOP	Perceived influence had positive effect on satisfaction, while ESOP account value had no significant effect.
9. French and Rosenstein 1984	Survey of 560 employees in firm with direct ownership	Ownership stake Perceived influence in job and co.	Perceived influence had positive effect on satisfaction, while ownership stake had no significant effect.

TABLE 2: ORGANIZATIONAL COMMITMENT/IDENTIFICATION UNDER EMPLOYEE OWNERSHIP

Authors of the studies	Source of data	Explanatory variables	Main results
Comparisons between employee-owners and non-owners			
1. Hammer, Stern, and Gurdon 1982	Surveys of 233 employees in 2 firms save by employee buyouts, 1-2 years after buyouts, 1976-77	Ownership status Ownership stake	Ownership stake positively linked to commitment; owners had higher commitment than non-owners for prdn. workers in one firm and non-prdn. workers in other firm, but similar levels among other workers.
2. Keef 1994	Survey of 105 middle managers in New Zealand financial institution, 1988	Ownership of stock Sale of stock	Those who purchased and held onto public stock, and those who had purchased but later sold it, had higher commitment than non-owners.
3. Long 1978b, 1980	Survey of 87 employees 6 mos. after 70% bought trucking co., and at knitting mill w/30% owners	Ownership status	Higher integration, involvement, commitment for owners, but no interaction with perceived participation
4. Oliver 1984	Survey of 40 employees in 6 Scottish co-ops, compared to population norms, 1981	Co-op membership	Commitment significantly higher than population norms on all three measures, even though wages below average. Workers cited cooperative structure as important in choice of workplace.
5. Rhodes and Steers 1981	Surveys of 141 employees in one U.S. plywood co-op and one conventional firm	Co-op membership	Higher commitment in co-op firm; commitment positively predicted by perceived participation in decisions and better group norms.
6. Russell et al. 1979	Surveys of 165 employee-owners in 6 U.S. refuse collecting firms, compared to 541 non-owners, 1977	Ownership status	Owners had higher organizational commitment on one measure, but similar commitment on another measure.
Pre/post comparisons			
7. Long 1982	Three surveys of 147, 184, and 248 employees, first one prior to employee purchase of Canadian electronics firm, 1979	Employee buyout after first survey Ownership stake	Commitment and trust up for those perceiving increased participation, but unchanged for those perceiving no change in participation. No relation to ownership stake.
8. Tucker et al. 1989	Two surveys of 38 and 39 employees at fast-growing small U.S. firm, 1982-84	ESOP adoption after first survey	Commitment up (but sample too small for significant results)
Comparisons within groups of employee-owners			
9. Buchko 1993	Survey of 218 employees in an ESOP company, 1987	ESOP account value Perceived influence from ESOP ESOP satisfaction Job satisfaction	Perceived influence, ESOP satisfaction, and job satisfaction had positive effects on commitment, while ESOP account value had no direct effect but did have indirect effect through ESOP satisfaction
10. French and Rosenstein 1984	Survey of 560 employees in firm with direct ownership	Ownership stake Perceived influence in job and co.	Perceived influence had positive effect on org. identification, while ownership stake had no significant effect

TABLE 3: EMPLOYEE BEHAVIOR AND OTHER RESEARCH ON EMPLOYEE OWNERSHIP

Authors of the studies	Source of data	Explanatory variables	Explanatory variables	Main results
Employee Behavior				
1. Buchko 1992, 1993	Survey of 218 employees in an ESOP company, 1987	Turnover Turnover intention	Financial value of ESOP account Perceived influence from ESOP	Perceived influence decreased both turnover intention and subsequent turnover. ESOP account value had no direct effect, but indirect effect by increasing ESOP satisfaction.
2. Hammer et al. 1981	Attendance data from 112 employees in furniture co., before and after buyout in 1976	Absenteeism	Employee purchase of co. Ownership stake	No significant change in overall absenteeism after employee buyout, but decrease in "voluntary" absenteeism, especially where large capital stake.
3. Kruse 1984	Manufacturing co. with ESOP owning 52% of stock, 1981	Turnover Union grievances	ESOP termination	Turnover and grievance rates unchanged after company was sold (without worker vote or input).
4. Rhodes and Steers 1981	Surveys of 141 employees in 1 plywood co-op, 1 other company	Turnover Grievances Absenteeism Tardiness Injuries	Co-op membership	Lower turnover and grievances in co-op, no difference in accidents, but higher absenteeism and tardiness.
5. Rooney 1992	275 U.S. firms, 206 majority employee-owned through ESOP or cooperative	OSHA injury in 1985	Percent of stock held by employees, alone and with participation measures	Employee ownership with worker participation had lower injuries, but mixed results for measures individually
Other research				
6. Hochner and Granrose 1985	Survey of 943 supermarket employees facing shutdown	Pledge of $5000 for employee buyout of stores	Worker attitudes and characteristics	Entrepreneurial ideals (risk-taking, importance of ownership) and collective/participative ideals predicted willingness to pledge for employee buyout
7. Onaran 1992	3 small employee-owned firms, 7 other firms, all in Ohio	Inequality of income, wealth, decision-making, privileges, prestige, social interaction	Membership in employee-owned firm	Intra-firm inequality lower in employee-owned firms on most measures

TABLE 4: PRODUCTIVITY AND PROFITABILITY STUDIES OF U.S. ESOPs

Authors of the studies	Source of data	Dependent variable	Type of comparison*	# of coeffs. reported	% > 0	% t-stats. > +2	Avg. effect size**	Major findings
1. Bloom 1985	3235 U.S. public firms over 1971-81, 610 with ESOP at end	Sales/employees	Cross-sectional Adoption Post-adoption growth	45 56 11	0.00% 0.00% 0.00%	0.00% 0.00% 0.00%	4.30% 6.20% 1.00%	Positive but mostly insignificant effects of ESOPs
2. Dunbar and Kumbhakar 1992	213 U.S. public firms with ESOPs, 1981-85	Sales	Cross-sectional Adoption	6 6	0.00% 0.00%	0.00% 0.00%	22.90% 3.20%	Positive but mostly insignificant effects of ESOPs
3. Kruse 1988, 1992	2,976 U.S. public firms over 1971-85, 923 with ESOP at end	Sales/employees	Cross-sectional Adoption Post-adoption growth	36 32 20	0.00% 0.00% 0.00%	0.00% 0.00% 0.00%	3.50% 4.20% 0.60%	Mostly positive but insignificant effects of ESOP adoption
4. Kruse 1993	500 U.S. public firms over 1975-91, 190 with ESOP at end	Sales/employees Value added	Adoption Post-adoption growth	12 12	0.00% 0.00%	0.00% 0.00%	1.10% 0.00%	Mostly positive but insignificant effects of ESOP adoption
5. Kumbhakar and Dunbar 1993	123 public firms adopting ESOPs or profit-sharing plans, 1982-87	Sales	Post-adoption growth	4	0.00%	0.00%	2.20%	Positive, significant effects of ESOP of 1.8-2.7% per year that ESOP has been in existence
6. Mitchell et al. 1990	495 U.S. business units in public firms, 1983-86	Profitability Sales/employees	Cross-sectional Post-adoption growth	6 6	0.00% 0.00%	0.00% 0.00%	5.60% 0.40%	Positive significant effects of ESOPs on performance growth
7. Quarrey and Rosen 1986	45 ESOP and 292 non-ESOP firms, 1975-86	Sales/employees	Adoption Post-adoption growth					ESOP companies had faster growth of sales, employment after adoption, but higher sales employee growth only where employee participation was high
8. U.S. GAO 1986	111 firms adopting ESOPs in 1976-79, paired with non-ESOP firms	Profitability Value-added/labor expense	Adoption	8	25.0%	12.5%	-1.0%	Positive significant effect on performance only for adopters w/high participation in decs.
Overall				**260**	**83.8%**	**21.5%**		
* Type of Comparison:								
Cross-sectional (comparing ESOP and non-ESOP firms at one point in time)				93	90.3%	24.7%	5.3%	
Adoption (pre/post comparison of ESOP adoption, relative to non-ESOP firms)				114	81.6%	17.5%	4.4%	
Post-adoption growth (comparing ESOP and non-ESOP productivity growth after adoption)				53	77.4%	24.5%	0.6%	

** Effect sizes represent average estimated percent difference between ESOP and non-ESOP firms for cross-sectional comparisons, and between pre- and post-adoption for ESOP adopters. For post-adoption growth comparisons, the effect size represents the percentage point difference in the yearly growth rate (e.g., 0.6% would indicate a 1.6% compared to a 1.0% growth rate).

TABLE 5: OTHER PRODUCTIVITY AND PROFITABILITY STUDIES OF EMPLOYEE OWNERSHIP (EXCLUDING COOPERATIVES AND ESOPS ALONE)

Authors of the studies	Source of data	Dependent variable	Employee ownership	# of coeffs. reported	% > 0	% t-stats. > +2	Major findings
1. American Capital Strategies 1994	300 U.S. public firms with >10% employee ownership	Total returns on co. stock	Presence of employee-owned stock > 10%				Employee ownership index has exceeded most market averages in 1991-94 period
2. Blasi et al. 1994	6671 U.S. public firms, 621 w/employee-owned stock exceeding 5% of co. market value in 1990	Profitability levels (1990), change (1980-90)	Presence of employee-owned stock > 5% Percent owned by employees	91 8	0.00% 0.00%	0.00% 0.00%	Positive significant relation of of plan to performance levels and growth for small cos., not for large; no relation to ownership percentage
3. Cable and Fitzroy 1980	42 German firms with employee ownership or profit sharing, 1972-76	Value added	Workers' capital Total profits to workers	4 4	0.00% 0.00%	0.00% 0.00%	Positive significant effect in "high-participation" firms, but negative and significant in "low-participation" firms
4. Conte and Tannenbaum 1978	30 U.S. cos. with ESOPs or direct ownership, compared to industry averages	Profitability	Percent owned by employees Pct. employees in plan	2 2	0.00% 0.00%	0.00% 0.00%	Positive significant relation with percent owned by employees, but not with other measures
5. Conte and Svejnar 1988, 1990	40 U.S. firms, 23 with employee ownership	Value added	Presence of employee ownership Pct. owned by employees	10 20	0.00% 0.00%	0.00% 0.00%	Positive effect of employee ownership, but negative effect for pct. owned by employees
6. Fitzroy and Kraft 1986, 1987	62 German firms, 1977-79	Value added Return on capital	Workers' capital/ total capital	4	0.00%	0.00%	Mean value of ownership measure doubles the mean return on capital
7. Jones and Kato Forthcoming	109 Japanese firms over 1973-80, majority with an ESOP at some point	Sales/employee	Adoption, presence of ESOP Interacted with bonus	0 20	0.00% 85.0%	0.00% 20.0%	ESOP adoption linked to 4-5% increase in productivity 3-4 yrs. after adoption; interacts positively with cash bonus
8. Lee 1989	50 Swedish employee-owned firms plus 51 conventional firms, 1983-85	Total Factor productivity Value added	Presence of ee. ownership Membership/L Profit sharing Workers' capital/L Interactions w/L	4 21 20 20 45	25.0% 38.1% 100.0% 10.0% 51.1%	0.0% 0.0% 35.0% 0.0% 0.0%	No general differences for employee-owned firms or features, either directly or through interactions with labor stock
9. Livingston and Henry, 1980; Brooks et al. 1982	51 U.S. cos. with stock purchase plans begun 1916-66, plus 51 other cos.	Profitability	Presence of stock purchase plan	90	0.0%	0.0%	Companies with stock purchase plans for at least 10 years had lower average profitability ratios
10. Mitchell et al. 1990	495 U.S. business units in public firms, 1983-86	Profitability Sales/employees	Presence of stock option plan	12	100.0%	8.3%	Positive but insignificant relation of stock option plans to performance